"If you are serious a[bout the enneagram, this] book is for you! Fin[ding our strengths, not our] weaknesses, is not a[n easy task. The enne-]gram work by Drew [is exceptional. I rec-]ommend this new a[ddition to our reliable] and smart enneagram wisdom."

Suzanne Stabile, author, *The Path Between Us*; coauthor, *The Road Back to You*; host of The Enneagram Journey podcast

"Drew resists the faddish enneagram-talk that tells people who they are, instead inviting each of us on a journey of discernment, exploring every obstacle to becoming our true selves, uncovering our unlived lives, and discovering our hidden vocation. This immensely practical gift holds the possibility of transformation, for yourself and for a hungry and hurting world. Savor it!"

Dr. Chuck DeGroat, author, *When Narcissism Comes to Church*; Professor of Pastoral Care and Christian Spirituality at Western Theological Seminary; therapist, spiritual director

"Drew writes on the enneagram with both clarity and conviction, not as a mere spectator gleaning from the sidelines, but a journeyman who has traveled the road thoroughly and brought back wisdom to share. I highly recommend this book to the enneagram student."

AJ Sherrill, lead pastor, Mars Hill Bible Church, author, *The Enneagram for Spiritual Formation*

"In this work, Drew has curated a wonderful tour for how the enneagram can helpfully guide us all to deeper exploration of vocation, calling, and life passion. Drew's writing style—like his teaching style—is both accessible and deep. New and long-time students of the enneagram will find gifts of wisdom in Drew's pages."

Hunter Mobley, enneagram teacher with Suzanne and Joe Stabile's Micah Center in Dallas, Texas; Nashville-based pastor and attorney; author, *Forty Days on Being a Two*

"This is a brilliant book! If you want to know and experience the life you desire to live, *The Enneagram of Discernment* delivers a map to get from here to there. You can read this book all at once but take your time. Dr. Drew's work with college students, along with his keen intellect, palpable empathy, and instinctual wisdom, serves as a GPS for young and old alike. Savor the landscape. Search your inner terrain, the heights, depths, and breadth of your soul with Drew as a faithful guide to help you discover more of the magnificent life you are meant to live."

Rev. Clare Loughrige, co-author, *Spiritual Rhythms of the Enneagram*; pastor at Crossroads Church (Marshall, MI); spiritual director

"Drew does a remarkable job of establishing separation between type and person while also writing about each type in such a way that we are all sure to be deeply seen. I appreciated the way he spoke of my dominant type (Seven) from a deep and nuanced perspective. In addition, he was able to offer tangible mindset shifts for working with the enneagram that take the information from understanding into application. I'm excited for you to start or continue your enneagram journey with *The Enneagram of Discernment* in your tool belt."

Sarajane Case, founder, @enneagramandcoffee; author, *The Honest Enneagram*

"*The Enneagram of Discernment* is an essential resource in the journey of self-discovery. Dr. Moser has accomplished what few others have in his ability to detail the extensive landscape of our human experience in a beautifully complex yet practically uncomplicated manner. His deft capacity to effectively guide each of us as we navigate past the shallowness of personality typing into the depths of true personal exploration can not be understated. This resource is a life-giving map for all of us seeking wisdom via practical applications in our efforts to discover our unique purpose."

Dr. Jerome D. Lubbe, author, *The Brain-Based Enneagram: You are Not a Number*

"Drew invites us to step past the shallow earth of simple self-awareness into the wider world of wholeness. This book is more than a map to flourishing. It's an excavation of the soul. Let

Drew's kind, practical wisdom guide you to the gift of coming home to who you really are."

KJ Ramsey, licensed professional counselor; author, *This Too Shall Last: Finding Grace When Suffering Lingers*

"On the surface, 'discernment' is about answering the occasional pressing question: 'What should I do?' However, with profound depth, clarity, and insight, *The Enneagram of Discernment* shows us how cultivating discernment is more essentially about braving with tenderness and vulnerability the sacred space of our authentic selfhood—and doing this as a devoted practice each and every day of our 'wild and precious' lives. If you are feeling lost, uncertain, or confused, Dr. Moser will help direct you to the trailhead of your own identity and gently offer you a map home."

Rev. Nhiên Vương, founder, Evolving Enneagram; International Enneagram Association accredited professional; ordained interspiritual minister

"*The Enneagram of Discernment* has quickly become one of the top resources we recommend for people wanting to use the ancient wisdom of the enneagram for its intentioned purpose of liberation. Drew's unique take on cultivating discernment through the enneagram provides a much-needed accessibility to an intimidating subject. This book not only provides a map but also the wisdom and guidance from the heart of a teacher who kindly and thoughtfully leads you each step of the way on the journey of finding your identity, purpose, and direction. We are thankful for Drew's gift to the conversation and believe you will be as well."

Rebekah TenHaken, co-founder and Director of Content and Collaboration for *Enneagram Magazine*

"With the acumen of a scholar, the heart of a servant-leader, and the wisdom of a sage, Drew Moser has created a landmark book. *The Enneagram of Discernment* is deeply rooted in tradition while simultaneously weaving fresh, illuminating insights on identity, vocation, wisdom, and practice. Whether you're a seasoned student of the enneagram or just being introduced to this ancient tool for holistic transformation, there is no better companion for deepening your journey into the true self. This book is sure to stand the test of time and belongs on the shelf alongside the great contemporary enneagram teacher."

Ryan Kuja, writer, spiritual director, & author, *From the Inside Out: Reimagining Mission, Recreating the World*

"If you are new to the enneagram or an enneagram expert, this book will speak to you. Drew Moser has written an inspired book! Drew's lifelong passion for helping young people discern their pathway in life has been transformed into a guide for us all. Drew clearly and skillfully uses the fundamental tenets of the enneagram to help us see and uncover our authentic selves. This allows us to listen and respond to the wisdom of a deeper calling. Challenging and meaningful questions and exercises at the end of chapters help us find a felt sense of what we are discovering and takes this wonderful information from head knowing to a full body, heart and head understanding. Like Drew, I have a literal room full of books on the enneagram. I have multiple copies of my favorite books and those I find most helpful, to lend to clients, students and friends. Rest assured there will be multiple copies of *The Enneagram of Discernment* in my library!"

Nan Henson, International Enneagram Association Accredited Professional, Riso-Hudson Certified Teacher & Authorized Workshop Leader; founding board member of IEA Georgia; owner, Enneagram Atlanta

"When it comes to exploring our vocation—or helping others do the same—many leaders feel ill-equipped. We're desperate for resources that go beyond navel-gazing, pop-psychologizing, or slapping a spiritual shellac on standard decision-making advice. *The Enneagram of Discernment* does none of this. Instead, it invites us to look inward in a new way—to take a trip to the center of ourselves, not only to better our understanding, but ultimately to see the *Imago Dei*. For those who want to apply the ancient enneagram tool to our output in today's world, Drew Moser is a humble, encouraging, and incredibly insightful guide. This book has the power to transform anyone who is willing to embark on the discernment journey!"

Erica Young Reitz, author, *After College*; founder and Principal, After College Transition

"Drew Moser's *The Enneagram of Discernment* is beautifully written, powerfully engaging, and rich in its depth! At a time when 'thrown together' enneagram books are flooding the marketplace, Drew Moser has come forth with a solid and authentic piece of work—a genuine contribution to the enneagram field. *The Enneagram of Discernment* offers a framework for working with the enneagram that keeps the true purpose of the enneagram alive throughout the book by staying true to a focus on using the enneagram for 'doing the Work' as opposed to a focus on the enneagram itself. The Type Chapters present a fresh view of each enneagram type from an 'inside out' perspective —describing more the experience of each Type than the typical 'outside in' descriptions of characteristics and behaviors. The exercises and practices offered throughout the book are purposeful and practical invitations for inquiry, one of the most effective tools for real and lasting personal and spiritual growth. I highly recommend this book to those new to the enneagram as well as to seasoned enneagram journeyers. Thank you, Drew, for this enneagram gem!"

Lynda Roberts, Riso-Hudson certified enneagram teacher, past president, International Enneagram Association, Accredited Professional, www.enneagramhorizons.com

"I have long considered my work with students at Christian colleges as 'standing at the crossroads' with them as they discern their futures, settle important questions about who they are and determine the purpose for their lives. In this volume, Drew Moser has developed an elegant and useful articulation of insights from the enneagram that will help me guide students in these crucible moments of their growth. For the reader who is new to the enneagram, Drew points out basic insights. For the seasoned pilgrim, he extracts and weaves together the concepts of vocation, wisdom and practice, thus helping any reader of any enneagram type to develop discernment. This is a book to which I will return often, for myself and as a recommended resource for students, colleagues, and leaders."

Dr. Edee M. Schulze, Vice President for Student Life at Westmont College (CA)

"As the enneagram has grown in popularity, it has unfortunately often been treated as a static personality profile, leaving unaccessed its greatest gifts for our evolution. But Drew's book is one of the rare ones that grasps and shares the dynamic power of this tool for our transformation as we confront the most challenging questions of vocation and discernment. With Drew's expert guidance, we can use the enneagram to pursue our best work and our truest lives."

Jason Adam Miller, founder and Lead Pastor, South Bend City Church (IN)

"This book beautifully unpacks how better understanding ourselves through the enneagram can lead us on a path of discernment. The nine questions serve as practical tools that nurture wisdom in making good life decisions."

Dr. Kris Hansen-Kieffer, Vice Provost for Student Success and Engagement at Messiah College (PA)

"This is not just another enneagram book, like many of them out there, regurgitating what was written in the first books. Drew's approach is unique in its depth and practicality, giving readers a fresh approach to understanding the 'why' of type and the 'how' of practicing loosening our addictive patterning to reclaim our innate capacity for wisdom needed to flourish where we are."

Seth Abram, enneagram writer/teacher, @integratedenneagram; Nashville-based singer/songwriter, co-host, Fathoms | An Enneagram Podcast

"Dr. Drew Moser is a national leader in defining the struggles that the 20-something generation is going through and moreover, how to overcome those struggles. His new book on the enneagram is his best work helping people understand their type and how to best use knowledge of that type to live abundantly. As someone in his 50s, I learned a lot from Moser's brilliant work on the enneagram. Thus, I trust that people of all ages will learn and grow from reading this fantastic title. Moser notes that in a world of beauty, we often listen to our earbuds and social media. He astutely asks, 'What are we tuning out?' I encourage you to tune in to Moser's book and learn about how to live a more authentic life through discernment and hearing the voice of God."

Dr. John D. Foubert, dean and professor, College of Education, Union University (TN)

"Knowing and being able to integrate the enneagram's wisdom with my journey of discernment over the past two years was a gift just as Drew Moser describes it to be: to decide and live from the wholeness of the claim 'This is who I am.' That others can experience that integration because of Drew's work here is a similar gift! The enneagram is meant for so much more than trendy Facebook posts and Instagram pics. With *The Enneagram of Discernment*, we are taken into the 'so much more' in a rich, comprehensive, yet exceedingly clear and helpful way. Would you expect anything less from a college professor who's spent his years walking alongside young adults in the pursuit of their vocation? No doubt I will recommend this work again and again to those I serve of all ages."

Dr. David A. Bell, Executive Director of Circle City Fellows (Indianapolis, IN); founder of Enneagram Insight

"Understanding the way forward involves a willingness to experience self-awareness and a desire for transformation. *The Enneagram of Discernment* offers an invitation for both of these to take place through wisdom and practice. The integration of theory and reflection are intertwined in a thorough way through this insightful resource. Drew emulates a life of discernment through his own evolution of transformation."

Dr. Julia Hurlow, author, *Transcendence at the Table*; Director of Discipleship, Taylor University (IN)

"Discernment is one of those things that we all think we have finally obtained at one point in our lives. When in reality, we soon realize that this difficult & precarious balancing act, only dares us to continue confronting the ways in which we see, perceive and believe. Drew has skillfully and efficiently conveyed the deep wisdom of the enneagram in which, every fathom you descend you feel more and more at home in your body, soul, & mind. Drew has managed to gracefully hold in tension, the complexities of you, while still giving you access to the practicality of this ancient system."

Seth Creekmore, experiential enneagram teacher/musician; co-host, Fathoms | An Enneagram Podcast

"Each of us makes seemingly unimportant decisions every day and then every so often a monumental life decision must be made. This book harnesses the power of authentic self-discovery through the enneagram and provides an invitation into wisdom to discern life's decisions. Dr. Drew Moser is a gifted educator whose words will adeptly guide readers into a deeper understanding and application of the enneagram."

Dr. Amy VanDerWerf Carroll, Senior Consultant for Student Success at Credo

"The Enneagram of Discernment is an invitation to tend to your soul. While there's no shortage of resources on the enneagram, none marry story-telling, education, and reflective questions the way this book does so beautifully. Drew created a rare gift that we'll get to open over and over again."

Manda Carpenter, Jesus-follower, foster care advocate, & author, *Space: An Invitation to Create Sustainable Rhythms of Work, Play, and Rest*

"As the enneagram gains in both popularity and knowledge, it can easily become a fad or parlor trick—a tragedy for such a needed and time-tested tool. Thankfully, Drew Moser pushes the conversation forward, moving us beyond knowing our enneagram type and revealing how we can become more loving people through discerning how to deepen and develop as humans. If you want to go deep, The Enneagram of Discernment is a powerful way to do it."

Sean Palmer, author, *40 Days of Being a Three*

"I really enjoyed reading this book! Drew has not only captured the types in very accurate ways but he has also given people a map of how to use the enneagram in their lives. I have a new enneagram book to recommend to my clients that I trust and that is effective for deep personal growth."

Milton C. Stewart, certified enneagram and career coach; creator and host, Do It for the Gram: An Enneagram Podcast

THE ENNEAGRAM OF DISCERNMENT
(TYPE 4 EDITION)

The Enneagram of Discernment:
The Way of Vocation, Wisdom, and Practice (Type 4 Edition)

Drew Moser, Ph.D.

Foreword by Dr. Chuck DeGroat

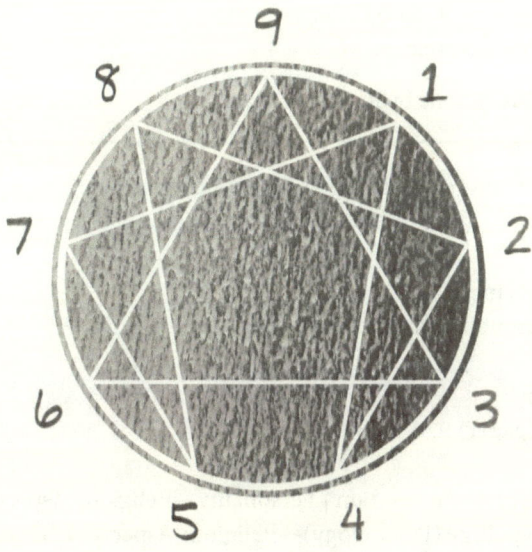

Falls City Press

THE ENNEAGRAM OF DISCERNMENT (TYPE 4 EDITION)
The Way of Vocation, Wisdom, and Practice

© 2021 Falls City Press by Drew Moser

2108 Seventh Avenue
Beaver Falls, PA 15010
www.fallscitypress.com

All rights reserved. Except for brief quotations in printed reviews, no part of this book may be reproduced, stored, or transmitted by any means without prior written permission of the publisher.

All websites listed herein are accurate as of the date of publication but may change in the future. The inclusion of a website does not indicate the promotion of the entirety of the website's content.

All rights reserved.

Cover Design by Rafetto Creative
www.rafettocreative.com

Interior Illustrations by Rachel Aupperle

Library of Congress Cataloging-in-Publication Data

Moser, Drew, 1979—

    p. cm.
Includes bibliographical references.

Identifiers:
  ISBN: (paper) 978-0-7369184-3-2

Subjects: LCHS: Enneagram | Personality—Religious Aspects—Christianity | Typology (Psychology)—Religious Aspects   I. Title.

BV4597.62.M79 2020

Printed in the USA

Dedication

To all the brave souls in search of a deeper and better way...

To those in search of greater clarity, awareness, and wisdom...

To those with a holy discontent living in a world increasingly frenetic, tiring, isolating, and polarizing...

...this book is for you.

I wish I could share a cup of coffee and talk about these things with each of you. Alas, this will have to suffice. I hope it helps.

One step at a time, together.

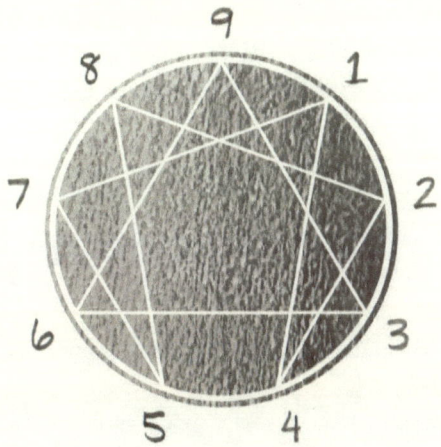

Contents

Foreword xvii

Author's Note xix

Introduction: This is Who I Am 1

Chapter 1: The Enneagram and Barriers to Discernment 17

Chapter 2: The Vocation Triad: Identity, Purpose, & Direction ... 37

Chapter 3: The Wisdom Triad: Doing, Feeling, Thinking 59

Chapter 4: The Practice Triad: Past, Present, Future 91

What I Mean When I Say 113

Chapter 5: Type Four: "The Individualist" 115

Conclusion: Living the Way of Discernment 135

Acknowledgments 143

Appendix: The Nine Questions of The Way of Discernment 147

Appendix: Five Axioms of Discernment 149

Appendix: Enneagram Settling Statements 153

Appendix: Nine Tips for Enneagram Typing 155

Appendix: The Nine Identity Statements of the Enneagram 157

Appendix: Nine Stages of Enneagram Learning 159

Appendix: Recommended Enneagram Resources 163

FOREWORD

At 50, I look back at my life and see distraction, fragmentation, confusion, and reactivity. Even as one committed to spiritual disciplines and interior silence, I've too-often bounced upon the waves, without a mooring. As a result, I've found myself exhausted, grumpy, and sometimes desperate. Can you relate?

In the late 1990s, a wise guide provided a helpful map for me in the Enneagram, a tool with ancient roots, yet one crafted for contemporary challenges. This tool, with great precision, named certain adaptive patterns in my life, coping mechanisms that locked me into self-sabotaging habits. Given its relative obscurity in my Christian community, I pieced together an Enneagram-education of my own, using the tool in my pastoral work and in my clinical counseling practice. I taught a class for a seminary on vocation featuring the Enneagram as the central wisdom-tool for discernment and practice. In every realm, it proved helpful. In my own life, it proved transformational.

And then, as I often say, the Enneagram got sexy. With an evangelical and pop-psychology makeover, this tool, which once lurked in the shadows, became mainstream, through a flurry of books, in podcasts, through social media Ennea-influencers, and more. Suddenly, this wisdom tool became another quick-fix strategy. I was receiving phone calls to help evangelical church staffs fix their relationship problems through half-day Enneagram seminars. But with growing attention came growing suspicion. Those suspicious of this new tool outlawed its use in some circles. Discouraged, I stopped teaching it and talking about it for a while.

And yet, I'm beginning to see new, wise-and-seasoned engagements with the Enneagram. Engagements like the book you're holding right now. Drew resists the faddish Enneagram-talk that tells people who they are. Instead, he invites each of us on a journey of discernment, exploring every obstacle to becoming our true selves, uncovering our unlived lives, and discovering our hidden vocations. He takes up the ancient task once again, offering the Enneagram not as the easy-fix or instant-remedy, but as wisdom for the journey—a time-honored tool for discernment.

Drew writes, "Discernment is the gift and practice of living our lives from a deep sense of vocation, with wisdom, in the fullness of time." And are we not all eager for discernment in a world that seems more chaotic and lives that feel more fragmented by the day?

Years ago, the sage Evelyn Underhill wrote, "Vocation is a gradual revelation—of me, to myself, by God—it is who we are, trying to happen." This is also true of the broader gift and practice of discernment. Drew invites you into this gradual revelation, providing a map with trails to follow, questions to ponder, and practices to engage. He trusts that God, who dwells at the center of your being, whispers this wisdom and leads the way. He believes that you are God's image-bearer, born to flourish, designed for significance and meaning and impact in your world.

This immensely practical gift holds the possibility of transformation, for yourself and for a hungry and hurting world. Drew has written it in a spiritually hospitable way: Readers from any faith tradition (or no faith tradition) will find it helpful. But it doesn't promise an easy path. Drew asks you, the reader, to commit to engaging it with your whole selves—not just heads, but hearts and bodies. If you're ready, this wise companion for your journey will take you into the profound depths of your own heart and into the deep needs of our hurting world. Savor it.

Dr. Chuck DeGroat
Author, *When Narcissism Comes to Church: Healing Your Community from Emotional and Spiritual Abuse*; Professor of Pastoral Care and Christian Spirituality at Western Theological Seminary; therapist, spiritual director

AUTHOR'S NOTE

The enneagram is ancient and open source, which often puts it at odds with our modern world of intellectual property. Many teachers have left their mark through trainings, books, articles, and the like. They are right to be mindful of how their content is being used by others. I've had good friends warn me about entering my own writing into the fray. Writing something new about the enneagram can be stepping into a mine field. Since Claudio Naranjo began teaching the enneagram in Berkeley, California, there have been hundreds of books, countless schools, institutes, trainings, conferences, podcasts, and the list goes on.

I've noticed a tension between two approaches to enneagram writing. The first approach fails to properly recognize (in citations and references) source material. A lack of citations implies that everything in a resource is of the author's own creation. We all learn from others, so this seems silly. The second approach is to cite whenever and wherever possible, which to some in the enneagram community implies a lack of originality. As a trained scholar and academic, my inclination is to build upon the good work of others. I can't bring myself to the first approach, and I disagree with those who look down upon the second. In my guild, citations and references convey honor and respect, meant to communicate that others' work is important enough to remain in the conversation. I hope those I cite feel honored that their work is influential to others. I've been tediously careful in trying to note where I sourced material and tried to let the reader know when I chart my own path with the content.

In general, my own enneagram training comes in a few forms. I've sat at the feet of some of the best enneagram teachers in intensive workshop environments. This book stands on their shoulders. As a scholar, another important mode of training comes from research. My own ever-expanding enneagram library bolsters my learning, and you'll see references to it throughout these chapters. I'm also active in the International Enneagram Association, and have learned much from my peers in workshops, conversations, and digital communication. In today's age, social media is ubiquitous, and beyond the memes and gifs can be found some truly profound content from enneagram friends around the world. All to say, I turned over as many rocks as possible in the enneagram world and did my best to let you know what I found. Thanks in advance for your grace and understanding.

In the complete edition of **The Enneagram of Discernment**, I offer 350 pages of insight into how our personalities help and hinder our decision-making. The complete edition includes a chapter for each Type, and the response by readers has been overwhelmingly positive. Many have also expressed a desire for a version of *The Enneagram of Discernment* that is less, shall we say, comprehensive and more focused on one's dominant type.

My publisher and I thought that was a great idea, and we've created type-specific editions for each of the nine enneagram types. We created this option in hopes of making the content of *The Enneagram of Discernment* as accessible and manageable as possible. Enjoy!

Introducing the Way of Discernment

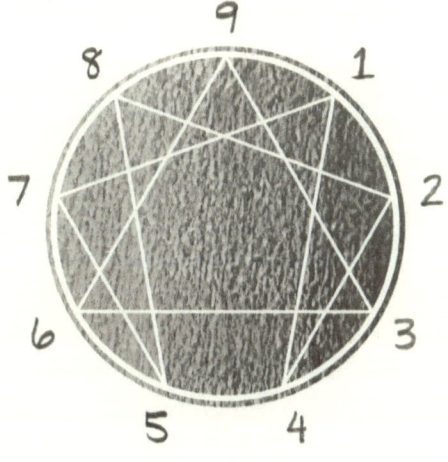

Introducing the Way
of Discernment

INTRODUCTION
This is Who I Am

"Do I contradict myself? Very well, then I contradict myself.
I am large, I contain multitudes."
—Walt Whitman

This is not who I am. The words were in response to the firestorm surrounding Philadelphia Eagles running back LeSean McCoy in a tragic 2013 twitter spat with an ex-girlfriend.[1] After first claiming his Twitter account was hacked, McCoy finally owned up to his actions, and issued an apology statement.

This is not who I am. The now infamous University of New Mexico women's college soccer player Elizabeth Lambert expressed deep regret when a 2009 video went viral showing her dragging an opponent to the ground by her ponytail. "I look at it and I'm like, 'That is not me,'" said Lambert.[2]

This is not who I am. A freshman Chi Omega sorority member at American University thump-tapped the sentence in an Instagram post apologizing for using the "n-word" in a video filmed by another sorority sister.[3]

This is not who I am. The legendary professional wrestler/entertainer Hulk Hogan invoked the phrase when an audio transcript surfaced in 2015 in which Hogan used racial slurs in a conversation with his daughter.[4]

This is not who I am. The sentence was invoked yet again in 2019 by then Virginia Governor Ralph Northam after old racist yearbook photos came to light.[5]

This is not who I am. When a leader or celebrity gets sideways with the public, lawyers and public relations firms swoop in to manage the crisis. Apparently these six words are standard boiler plate apology language used to deescalate the situation. In each instance, they are meant to convey an incongruence of past decisions made and the true character of a person.

And every time a statement is released or a remorseful person utters them in a press conference, the collective reaction is almost always the same: *that's not a real apology. We teach our children to give better apologies than that.*

It's a fair critique, because it truly is a terrible apology. It's an attempt to prove that while I own up to my mistakes, this one time was an aberration. It's an effort in diminishing the disaster to minimize the damage. Each time such bad apologies are offered, the temptation is to roll our eyes and mutter: *You're not sorry.*

Here's the thing: each time a person shuffles to a microphone at a press conference and implores to the masses that *this is not who I am*, I now think about the situation differently. I still see it for the contrived charade that it often is. I still hear the formulaic, crafted message. I still sense the inadequacy of the "apology." But along with it, I now have a different response. When someone claims that *this is not who I am*, I think:

You're exactly right.

Our decisions have the powerful role in forming and representing who we are. These apologies at least acknowledge the interconnectedness of our identity (being) and our decisions (doing). Such public failures remind me that on the other side of my sanctimony is a recognition that I too struggle with the idea of who I am, and make decisions that feel incongruent. I also find myself in situations in which, with hindsight, I feel regret or remorse about the encounter. At the risk of projection, I'd say we all do. The human experience is full of dissonance, where our behaviors seem mismatched with who we want to be.

And it's a uniquely human issue. The poet-philosopher David Whyte reminds us that: "We are the only creation that refuses to be ourselves."[6] We seem to be plagued by a collective identity crisis. Psychologist David Benner agrees: "In all of creation, identity is a challenge only for humans. A tulip knows exactly what it is. It is never tempted by false ways of being. Nor does it face complicated decisions in the process of becoming."[7]

I'm not claiming that celebrity apologies convey the full weight of our identity issues. But I think they point to it, even if unbeknown to the celebrity. It's a glimpse of the internal tug of war we all wage: the battle between a *persona* and an authentic self. Our inability to grapple with identity leads us to make poor decisions. They may not be for the world to see, but they are poor decisions nonetheless. Our struggles with identity also significantly inhibit our ability to make decisions altogether. Left unchecked, we can come to a place of poverty (of wisdom) and paralysis (of action). When faced with life's decisions, we need both wisdom and right action.

We need to know who we truly are… and how to make good and wise decisions accordingly. Why is this so difficult? Why do we suffer from such confusion about who we are? There are probably a multitude of reasons, but three loom the largest:

1. We lie to ourselves, often for very understandable reasons.
2. We are overwhelmed, which inhibits our ability to live with congruence.
3. We've neglected our capacity to listen well, choosing to listen to the wrong voices.

Let's take each in turn.

We lie to ourselves. The Dutch Catholic priest Henri Nouwen wisely acknowledges our tendency for self-deceit, outlining the three lies of identity:[8] *I am what I do, I am what I have,* and *I am what others say about me.*

When we believe these lies, we live in some unhealthy ways. We devote ourselves to activities that aren't true to who we are. We collect material possessions in hopes that they bring a sense of fulfillment. We cling to the approval of others. Our minds, hearts, and bodies search and scan for an elusive form of validation and approval. When we feel we've failed at this, we turn to contriving schemes and tweaking formulas to craft a better persona, one that is perhaps more effective at these things.

We are overwhelmed. In addition, we are an overwhelmed bunch. We are overworked and overstressed. In our digital age, we are bombarded with information, we are consumed by work and stress, and we fail to slow down enough to listen to the wisdom within. Despite the promise of technology to make our lives easier, it often has the opposite effect. Rather than reducing our workload, it has increased it. Tending to emails outside of normal business hours is now the norm, not the exception. A study conducted by a Virginia Tech professor indicates that the mere expectation (regardless of the time we spend) to check work emails after business hours harms the health of employees and their families.[9]

We also tend to not use the paid time off we earn. A 2019 poll revealed that only 28% of Americans planned to max their vacation time.[10] The average American worker used, on average, only 54% of their time off. This is despite the many studies that prove the health benefits of taking time away from work.

A nice ending to this story would be to believe that, *The reasons we overwork are because we love it so much.* But other studies reveal that we aren't enjoying life as much as we hope. A global poll conducted by Gallup finds that Americans are among the most stressed people in the world.[11] And stress is increasing with each generation. Generation Z, those born after 1997, are the most "stressed out Generation in American history."[12]

And despite our perpetual digital connectivity, adults in America are lonely. Since 1985, the number of Americans who report having no close friends has tripled.[13] Living in a perpetual state of burnout, stress, and loneliness results in a lack of authentic identity void of any purpose and direction.

We aren't listening well. Most people I know who have committed to the difficult path of living a more authentic life often look back and can clearly see the signs, the voices, and the opportunities ignored or dismissed. And most, if honest, admit "I wasn't listening." Parker Palmer, in his profound book *Let Your Life Speak*, writes, "We listen for guidance everywhere except from within."[14] I work on a college campus, which affords me the opportunity to observe young adults and how they live. Ours is a sprawling, beautiful campus, full of trees and creeks and walking paths. And yet, such beauty and space can't compete with earbuds and social media. I often wonder, what are we listening to? Perhaps a better question: What are we tuning out?

Palmer implores us to listen to our lives, for they have something to say. This requires us to tune our listening differently, inwardly, tending to our soul.

He writes:

> The soul is like a wild animal—tough, resilient, savvy, self-sufficient, and yet exceedingly shy. If we want to see a wild animal, the last thing we should do is to go crashing through the woods, shouting for the creature to come out. But if we are willing to walk quietly into the woods and sit silently for an hour or two at the base of a tree, the creature we are waiting for may well emerge, and out of the corner of an eye we will catch a glimpse of the precious wildness we seek.[15]

In our current state, we don't have much time and space for soul work. Such inner work requires a different sort of listening. It requires a different pace of life. It requires an honesty with ourselves that can seem scary.

But to avoid who we truly are and continue living otherwise is actually scarier. If we lie to ourselves long enough, we start to forget what's true. We overwhelm ourselves and wonder if we can sustain the pace. We doubt our ability to listen, and wonder if we'll never be able to hear the right voices. Our persona gradually shifts from that which helps us feel a sense of comfort in our world to that which feels suffocating. To continue in our default patterns and settings will result in further confusion about our identity, further division within the various parts of our lives, and a diminishment of our purpose and direction.

We are desperate for discernment, searching for wisdom to make good decisions. This requires a sacred journey to authentic identity, demanding a different pace than our calendar apps typically allow. Workaholism, stress, and loneliness aren't very helpful places from which to make decisions. What would it look like to live free of them? What if we reconsidered the question, *What should I do with my life?*

May Sarton captures the journey well:

Now I become myself.
It's taken time, many years and places.
I have been dissolved and shaken,
Worn other people's faces...[16]

To know who we are and then live accordingly is not easy. The path to an authentic identity that makes wise decisions takes time, and we must acknowledge our prior efforts to wear "other people's faces." I used the word *persona* previously to discuss how we tend to live out of false places of identity. The Latin root for *persona* is "theatrical mask." The personas we present to the world are masks. In fact, it seems easier to live from persona and consider it identity. But we only put on the mask because we want to shape how others see us. It's a response to perception rather than reality. To live from an authentic sense of identity is a response to how I see myself.[17]

If you've ever worn a mask, you know that it often impedes your vision. Most costume masks have holes for your eyes, but even when you line your eyes up with the holes your vision is restricted. To live well requires that we name the masks that we wear, take them off, and then see our lives with more clarity, range, and depth. The initial glance can be tough, because it leads to the acknowledgement that "the life I am living is not the same as the life that wants to live in me."[18]

When we do this, we're beginning to scratch the surface of the essence of life. Mary Oliver, in her poem "The Summer Day," asks "Tell me, what is it you plan to do with your one wild and precious life?"[19]

It's a rich question, full of simplicity and complexity. Those that read it fall into two camps. The first camp is inspired. Oliver assumes that our lives are wild and precious. Our plans for life should honor the wildness and preciousness. Such "wild" living beckons us to adventure and anticipation. The second camp is anxious. *I don't know! That's what I'm trying to figure out!* A lack of plans cause many to worry that their lives will be a waste. Confusion, frustration, and even depression can creep in.

If we are willing to name the masks we wear, take them off, and explore what's underneath, we can carry the weight of inspiration and discovery Oliver gives, and make decisions accordingly. That is the essence of this book. We each desperately need to find the path back to our true selves, and then live from that place of identity to make wise decisions. By exploring the ancient wisdom of the enneagram, coupled with the gift and practice of discernment, we will. By becoming ourselves, we learn to discern our path with wisdom.

Discerning Identity, Discerning Life

To arrive at a point of authentic identity is rare. Most continue to live with the mask on. But for those who are willing to put in the work, a sacred space emerges. It's a place of raw vulnerability. It's a tender place, full of sensitivity, goodness, fear, and courage. Entering it can conjure two responses. The first is defensive, where we shame ourselves for our inadequacies and shortcomings, heaping criticism. This is engaging the space with *judgment*. We become our own worst enemy: an inner critic.

The second is hospitable, where we see ourselves as we truly are, and welcome with love. And to see is to love.[20] This is engaging the space with *discernment*.

The result of a shift from persona to identity is this ability to discern a wild and precious life. In your hands is no ordinary self-help book. The realm of discernment is too challenging for simplistic formulas. Nor is this your ordinary enneagram book, some of which tend to introduce the reader to recycled types and tips.

Instead, I hope to explore the ways in which the enneagram can illuminate the path to authentic identity, and in so doing, cultivate the wisdom to discern life's decisions, big and small. In short, I call it the **Enneagram of Discernment**; a framework of becoming ourselves so we can discern with wisdom. The tragic irony of our "information age" is that our unfettered access to information has failed to make us wiser. It fails to help those who confess: *This is not who I am*.

Imagine the shift from the brokenness of *This is not who I am* to the wholeness of living in such a way that you can claim *This is who I am*. To do so would allow us to get out of some unhelpful patterns of behavior. This is what discernment provides. To do so requires an integrity and authenticity saturated with wisdom, the holistic intelligence that guides us to effectively engage the many decisions of life. The enneagram invites us into how we can bring our full and authentic selves into the world with this sort of wisdom.

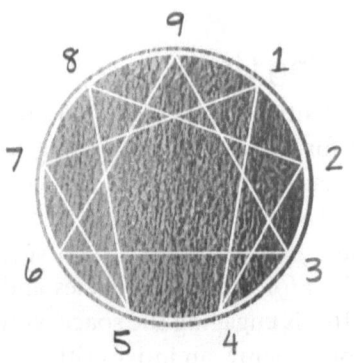

When the enneagram comes up at parties or other social settings, it's often discussed as a way to describe who people *ARE*. This is understandable, but unfortunate. The enneagram is truly about understanding who you are *NOT*. Through the awareness that comes with discovering your dominant type, one can begin to see our habitual patterns, behaviors, reactions, defenses, barriers and capacities.

If you're new to the enneagram framework and don't know your dominant type, no worries. Chapter One will be a helpful introduction. If you'd like help discovering your type before you read on, check out the appendices, which provide tips for typing and exercises to help you discover your type.

Discovering your dominant enneagram type is just the beginning. In this present surge in popularity of the enneagram, there are untold amounts of information out there, much of it being peddled by people eager to sell you their knowledge. Such fervor isn't all bad, but it risks creating a culture of superficiality. There's a lot of repackaged content about personality types out there. Discovering your personality type is merely the trailhead to a deep, complex, and important journey to self-discovery. It's the place we start, not the place we end. When working with the enneagram we must remember that:

INFORMATION < KNOWLEDGE < WISDOM

Any enneagram fan can master the enneagram of personality with enough information and knowledge. The Enneagram of Discernment invites us into wisdom and cultivates it. In order to discern who we are and what we should do, we have to plunge deeper. Information leads to simple formulas and knowledge simply gives us tools. The Enneagram of Discernment provides something much more profound. It provides a way that allows us to explore a crucial question:

How do we hold the map of our lives and make sense of it?

Introducing the Enneagram of Discernment

By drawing from the wisdom of the enneagram to cultivate the gift and practice of discernment, we can live from a grounded, working definition of discernment:

> *Discernment is the gift and practice of living our lives from a deep sense of vocation, with wisdom, in the fullness of time.*

Simply, discernment is applied identity. Wisdom comes from a place of authenticity, where we can approach challenging situations not just by looking at it, but beneath it and through it.[21] When we see through, we see what's truly at stake.

Hannah Anderson writes, "Discernment does not change the challenges we face; it changes our ability to face them."[22] This is where the wisdom of the enneagram engages the challenges of our lives.

What we need is a map. Like many 90s American teens, my Thursday nights revolved around the TV show *Friends*. In a memorable episode, the main characters took a trip to London, England. Joey, in an effort to find his way in this foreign land, opened up a paper map of London, placed it on the sidewalk, and literally stepped onto the map in an attempt to orient himself. Joey's friend Chandler was characteristically exasperated. The scene, while funny, conveys a profound truth: A map is only as good as your ability to hold it and make sense of it.[23]

The enneagram can provide a map of our lives, but we must learn to hold it and make sense of it. This is the enneagram work that is beneath simply understanding the nine personality types. This book is an invitation to discover your authentic self so that you can discern your life with wisdom.

The Enneagram of Discernment is a triadic map of applied identity:

- Triad 1—Vocation: the Divine Call of identity, purpose, and direction.
- Triad 2—Wisdom: the holistic intelligence that guides us to engage our lives with integrity and authenticity.
- Triad 3—Practice: our intentional work in the fullness of time.

Together the triads of discernment provide nine key questions of discernment:

Vocation

- Who am I?
- Why am I here?
- Where am I going?

Wisdom

- What am I thinking?
- What am I feeling?
- What am I doing?

Practice

- What am I remembering?
- What am I experiencing?
- What am I anticipating?

Each type has its own journey of discernment through these triads and questions. I must warn you that this journey isn't easy. This book will illuminate ways of transformation, but the process can be painful. In the words of David Benner, "No one should work with the enneagram if what they seek is flattery."[24] Surrendering our ego-centered[25] perspective on life can hurt. But it's also liberating.

In Chapter One, we'll explore the enneagram a bit more deeply and consider the three primary emotional barriers to discernment. For newcomers to the enneagram, this will provide enough context to make sense of the book. For those well-versed in the enneagram, we'll explore some new content on the triads and discernment.

In Chapter Two, we'll explore the first triad of the Enneagram of Discernment: Vocation. I'll unpack this ancient theological concept and remind us of our Divine Call to flourish in our identity, purpose, and direction. We'll walk through the shadows of the false self in pursuit of the true. From this place, we'll consider a more grounded purpose and direction.

In Chapter Three, we'll consider the Enneagram of Discernment's second triad: Wisdom. The cultivation of wisdom draws from the full range of intelligence available: head, heart, and body. We'll explore the enneagram's ancient wisdom of three centers of intelligence, which are now being corroborated with neuroscience.

In Chapter Four, we'll expand our understanding of time through the Enneagram of Discernment's third triad: Practice. By deepening our understanding of enneagram type, we can see how our egoic personality hinders our ability to live in the fullness of time: past, present, and future. We'll explore yet another helpful grouping of the enneagram: the stances.

Chapter Five considers how your specific type helps and hinders the process of discernment. This chapter will give additional type-specific content that sheds light on how the type digresses from a place of personality and will explore the way of discernment through the triadic map of applied identity.

I conclude the book with some encouragement and perspective to aid your lifelong cultivation of discernment. I also provide a number of helpful resources in the appendices for further study and exploration.

Each chapter concludes with exercises to aid you in your journey to discern life from authentic identity. In our present digital age, our brains have become accustomed to scanning and skimming as quickly as possible. Deep transformative work requires observation, time, and reflection. Savor this text. Take your time.

Finally, heed the words of Parker Palmer: "Inner work, though it is a deeply personal matter, is not necessarily a private matter: inner work can be helped along in community."[26] This journey requires intentional time alone and with others. Be sure to develop healthy rhythms of solitude and community that allow you to incorporate these ideas.

This is not who I am. It's a subpar apology. But with the wisdom of the Enneagram of Discernment, it's a powerful statement acknowledging our confused and distorted identity.

No longer. *This is who I am.* Time to hold the map of your life and make sense of it.

Notes

[1] Adam Wells, "LeSean McCoy's Twitter Account Deleted After Public Blowup with Ex-Girlfriend," *Bleacher Report*, last modified, January 28, 2018, accessed October 1, 2019, https://bleacherreport.com/articles/1503592-lesean-mccoys-twitter-account-deleted-after-public-blowup-with-ex-girlfriend.

[2] Jere Longman, "Those Soccer Plays, in Context," *The New York Times*, last modified November 17, 2009, accessed October 1, 2019, https://www.nytimes.com/2009/11/18/sports/soccer/18soccer.html.

[3] The Eagle News Staff, "Video circulates on social media of Chi Omega member saying racial slur," *The Eagle*, accessed Feb 29, 2020, https://www.theeagleonline.com/article/2020/02/video-circulates-on-social-media-of-chi-omega-member-saying-racial-slur.

[4] Colen Gorentein, "Hulk Hogan apologizes for 'n-word' audio: 'This is not who I am,'" *Salon*, last modified July 24, 2015, accessed October 1, 2019, https://www.salon.com/2015/07/24/hulk_hogan_apologizes_for_n_word_audio_this_is_not_who_i_am/.

[5] Ari Shapiro and Gene Demby, "Why Calls for Racial Dialogue So Rarely Lead to It," *NPR*, last modified February 3, 2019, accessed October 1, 2019, https://www.npr.org/2019/02/04/691427223/why-calls-for-racial-dialogue-so-rarely-lead-to-it.

[6] David Whyte interview with Krista Tippett, "The Conversational Nature of Reality," *On Being,* last modified, December 27, 2018, accessed Oct 1, 2019, https://onbeing.org/programs/david-whyte-the-conversational-nature-of-reality-dec2018/.

[7] David G. Benner, *The Gift of Being Yourself: The Sacred Call to Self-Discovery* (Downers Grove, IL: IVP Books, 2015), p. 16.

[8] Nouwen explores these three lies in a video series on YouTube, delivered in 1992. I think they are so profound that they are worth another look here. See Henri Nouwen, "Being the Beloved," https://www.youtube.com/watch?v=SFWfYpd0F18&app=desktop.

[9] Nouwen, "Being the Beloved," https://www.youtube.com/watch?v=SFWfYpd0F18&app=desktop.

[10] Megan Leonhardt, "Only 28% of Americans Plan to Max out Their Vacation Days This Year," *CNBC Make It*, last modified April 27, 2019, accessed Oct 1, 2019. https://www.cnbc.com/2019/04/26/only-28percent-of-americans-plan-to-max-out-their-vacation-days-this-year.html.

[11] Niraj Chokshi, "Americans are Among the Most Stressed People in the World, Poll Finds," *The New York Times*, last modified April 25, 2019, accessed Oct 1, 2019, https://www.nytimes.com/2019/04/25/us/americans-stressful.html#targetText=Americans%20are%20among%20the%20most%20stressed%20people%20in%20the,according%20to%20a%20new%20survey.&targetText=The%20data%20on%20Americans%20is,with%20just%2035%20percent%20globally.

[12] American Psychological Association, *Stress in America: Generation Z*, October 2018: https://www.apa.org/news/press/releases/stress/2018/stress-gen-z.pdf.

[13] General Social Survey data, https://gss.norc.org/.

[14] Parker J. Palmer, *Let Your Life Speak: Listening for the Voice of Vocation* (San Francisco: Jossey-Bass, 1999), p. 5.

[15] Ibid, p. 8-9.

[16] May Sarton, "Now I Shall Become Myself," in *Collected Poems, 1930-1993* (New York: W.W. Norton & Company, 1993).

[17] David Benner's work deeply informed this perspective.

[18] Palmer, *Let Your Life Speak*, p. 2.

[19] Mary Oliver, "The Summer Day," in *Devotions: The Selected Poems of Mary Oliver* (New York: Penguin Press, 2017).

[20] Frederich Beuchner wrote about this beautifully. See Frederich Buechner, *The Remarkable Ordinary: How to Stop, Look, and Listen to Life* (Grand Rapids: Zondervan, 2017), p. 33.

[21] Henri Nouwen, *Discernment: Reading the Signs of Daily Life* (San Francisco: HarperOne, 2015), p. 6.

[22] Hannah Anderson, *All That's Good: Recovering the Lost Art of Discernment* (Chicago: Moody Publishers, 2018), p. 25.

[23]My brilliant friend and enneagram teacher Annie Dimond introduced me to this language of "learning to hold the map." Check out her work on Instagram: @enneagramforwholeness.

[24]Benner, *The Gift of Being Yourself*, p. 63.

[25]By ego I mean a psychological concept that is one of the three parts of psychoanalytic theory (along with the id and the superego). This is how you have learned to identity yourself. This, when combined with our dominant enneagram type, forms the adapted self.

[26]Palmer, *Let Your Life Speak*, p. 92.

CHAPTER ONE

The Enneagram and Barriers to Discernment

*"If you can find a path with no obstacles,
it probably doesn't lead anywhere."*
—Frank A. Clark

The enneagram is a framework of nine pilgrimages of personhood. In its essence, it's that simple. But it's a simplicity of understanding who we are that comes while working though the complexity of life. Each person's enneagram journey contains profound questions of vocation, wisdom, and practice that comprise the Way of Discernment.

My take on the enneagram is different than much of what is out there in print and on podcasts. It's worth explaining what the enneagram is (and isn't). The reality is that there are a lot of "enneagrams" out there and I want to be clear about the one I'm using.

The name "enneagram" derives from two Latin and Greek words: figure (*gram*) and nine (*ennea*). Figures of nine things have been found throughout antiquity. The enneagram's is a complicated and sorted history, without a definitive narrative.[1]

The modern enneagram framework typically contains a circle with nine interconnected points, like this:

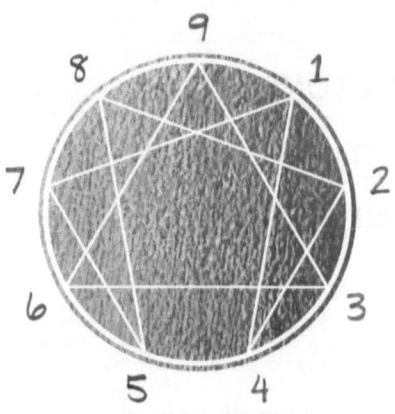

Recently, the enneagram has exploded in popularity, producing countless books, workshops, coaches, podcasts, and the like. Current use of the enneagram tends to fall into two camps. The first is primarily *psychological*, employing the enneagram as a personality typing tool; a handy way to understand people. In this way, the enneagram is compared to other typologies, such as the Myers-Briggs Type Indicator (MBTI), the Dominance influence Steadiness Conscientiousness Profile (DiSC), StrengthsFinder, etc. This use has been extended to social media (referred to by many as the "memefication" of the enneagram). In these instances, enneagram content takes on a digital pop-psychology tone. It risks becoming an object we consume, yet another opportunity to commodify one another.

The second realm of enneagram work is primarily spiritual, employing the enneagram as an esoteric tool—a means to enlightenment and spiritual transformation. This is why you'll find the enneagram used within mystical streams of every major religious tradition, as well as non-religious spiritualities. Used this way, the enneagram becomes an integral resource on the spiritual journey. This approach risks elevating the spiritual over our physicality.

With any resource, different understandings have their critics. Some find the psychological approach reductive and a departure from the enneagram's ancient roots. The enneagram only found its footing within the field of psychology in recent decades, and critics of "psychologizing" the enneagram point to its predation of modern psychology and the wisdom found beneath the "types." There's legitimate concerns about the shifts in enneagram content from an oral tradition to a written tradition and now to social media "content." Is it really appropriate to go to Instagram to find a series of posts on the best type of health smoothie for each type? For the purposes of discernment, which require time, reflection, and contemplation, digital spaces prove challenging, as they train our brains to merely skim and scan.[2]

Others find many offerings from the spiritual approach to esoteric and impractical, ignoring the important contribution modern psychology provides. Such critics scoff at "elitist" or "insider" tendencies within some spiritual camps in the Enneagram community. There are legitimate concerns in these spaces about privilege and practicality. Not everyone can afford to attend a seven-day spiritual retreat in luxury accommodations. And for those who can, connecting the experience to the everyday grind of life can be confusing.

The Enneagram of Discernment is an attempt to avoid the potential traps of both, offering invitations into the spirituality, psychology, and practicality that the enneagram provides. This maintains a sense of integrity when encountering the enneagram and the gift and practice of discernment.

With this approach in mind, a basic introduction is warranted. For the newcomers, consider this a crash course. For the ennea-savvy, consider this a return to the fundamentals.

A Way-Too-Brief-but-Still-Helpful Introduction to the Enneagram

- As mentioned above, the enneagram is a framework of nine pilgrimages of personhood.
- There are nine points (types) on the enneagram framework, with each point representing a particular persona. Each person has a dominant enneagram type that they lead with for the balance of their lives. Each person also contains aspects of all eight other types, but lead with

their one dominant type. All nine types have strengths and weaknesses. There is no hierarchy to the types.

- These types are labeled by numbers (1-9) and often by nicknames (more on these later). Your dominant type represents the set of habits and patterns you've developed over the course of your life to cope (in good and bad ways) in this world. It is your egoic personality; the character structure you've developed over time. Your egoic personality isn't necessarily a bad thing, but believing that this is identity leads to some unhealthy places. Many teachers refer to this as the "false self," or "adapted self." This is the *persona* that we put on to relate to others, express ourselves, defend ourselves, and survive.

- Your dominant "type" also helps you understand the ways in which you've lost sight of your authentic identity. Many teachers refer to authentic identity as the "true self" or "authentic self."

- The enneagram isn't really about behaviors. The enneagram is about core motivations and fears that drive certain behaviors. This distinguishes it from other typologies.

- The enneagram is perpetually triadic. Beyond a surface-level understanding of type lies a wealth of wisdom by grouping the ennea-types into various groups of three. These triads contain powerful wisdom for the pilgrimage. (Note: This book will explore a few of those triadic groupings.)

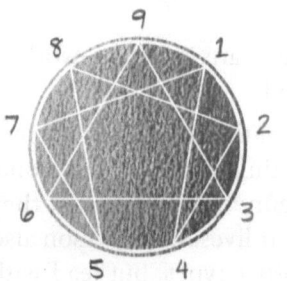

- The enneagram is a dynamic resource. While each person leads with a dominant type, the presence of the other eight types provides considerable movement throughout the framework. This is represented through the interconnected lines that traverse the circle. These inner dynamics represent how each type experiences stress and security. Each point on the circle has lines connecting it to two other types. One of those lines is the direction of stress (a coping mechanism) and the other is the direction of security (a place of safety, ease, and/or comfort)

- The enneagram is wonderfully simple, yet endlessly complex. It's tempting to read a short description of the nine types and believe you've figured everyone out. The reality is that to explore the enneagram with depth requires an acknowledgement that there is always more to learn and more to discover. This is because it is a dynamic framework, with opportunities for integration, disintegration, growth, maturity, and so much more. Thus, while each of us has a dominant type, we are so much more than our number.

The Nine Types of the Enneagram

There are many ways to introduce the nine types. For the Enneagram of Discernment, it's helpful to describe the types by what they truly want, not only what they too often settle for. These "wants" are core desires for each type. It's important to note that each of the type's "wants" are common to all, but explored in different ways. In other words, we all want these things, but the ways in which we go about them (and why) differ by type. It's here that each type's response to anxiety emerges. By anxiety, I mean the human response to stress in life. This is different than a clinically diagnosed anxiety disorder. Experiencing anxiety is a universal human phenomenon. Our responses to that anxiety vary by type. Each type's response results in a "settling," a settling for less than what we truly "want."

Granted, there are healthy ways to settle. But when our enneagram type settles, it tends to find a seemingly fixed default setting; one that is short of who we truly are. In the Enneagram of Discernment, it's helpful to be aware of a primary "want" that drives us, and the ways in which we typically "settle." (Remember: There is no hierarchy to the types, and each has its strengths and weaknesses.)

Type Eight ("The Challenger")—Type Eights want protection but settle for control.

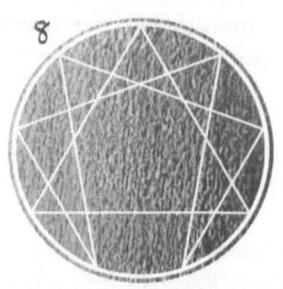

Type Eights are often labeled as "challengers." While this describes some common expressions of Eights, it doesn't capture what Eights are truly after. Eights, at their core, want protection. They want to be protected, and they want the world to be marked by protection. But when confronted with a world that isn't always protecting, the vulnerability feels threatening. They can see need for protection everywhere, and they see it most prominently within themselves. This leads Type Eights to feel anxious about life, and that stress manifests as a particular type of anger toward vulnerability: controlling their environment on their own terms. In order to keep the need for protection in check, Type Eights settle for the control they can manifest in their world. This pursuit of control can cause Eights to overlook the goodness of vulnerability in safe places.

Type Nine ("The Peacemaker")—Type Nines want peace but settle for calm.

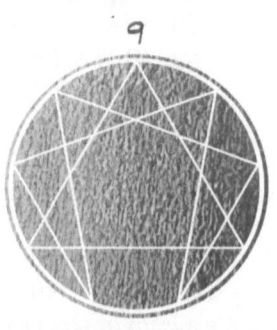

Type Nines are often labeled as "peacemakers." While this describes some common expressions of Nines, it doesn't capture all that Nines experience. Nines, at their core, want peace. They want peace within, and they want the world to be marked by peace. But when confronted with a world that isn't always peaceful, the vulnerability feels threatening. They can see need for peace everywhere, and they see it most prominently within themselves. This leads Type Nines to feel anxious about life, and that stress manifests as a particular type of anger toward disruption: passive aggression. In order to keep the need for peace in check, and to not disrupt with passive aggression, Type Nines settle for the calm they can maintain in their world. This pursuit of calm can cause Nines to forget themselves.

Type One ("The Reformer")—Type Ones want goodness but settle for order.

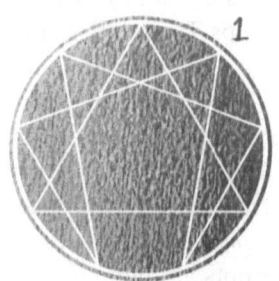

Type Ones are often labeled as "perfectionists." While this describes some Ones, it doesn't capture what Ones are truly after. Ones, at their core, want goodness. They want to be good, and they want the world to be good. But when confronted with a world that isn't always good, it feels like a consuming wrongness. They can see wrongness everywhere, and they see it most prominently within themselves. This leads Type Ones to feel anxious about life, and that stress manifests as anger. But because of their sensitivity to being good, they hold that anger down whenever possible. Anger then takes on a more subtle and acceptable version: resentment. In order to keep the resentment in check, Type Ones settle for order in their world: self-improvement, rules, a sense of fairness, a sense of being right, ordering their environment, etc. Little releases of resentment help to keep things in check. Small attempts at improvement aim to satisfy the pursuit of goodness.

Type Two ("The Helper")—Type Twos want unconditional love but settle for niceness.

Type Twos are often labeled as "helpers." While this describes some Twos, it doesn't capture what Twos are truly after. Twos, at their core, want love. They want to embody love, and they want the world to be marked by love. But when confronted with a world that isn't always loving, it feels like insufficiency.

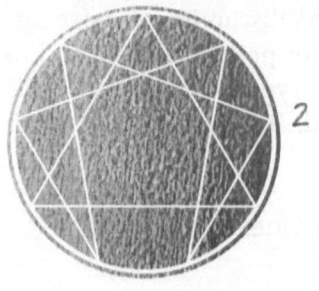

They can see need for love everywhere, and they see it most prominently within themselves. This leads Type Twos to feel anxious about life, and that stress manifests as shame. But because of their sensitivity to being loved, they hold that shame down whenever possible, and resolve it through focusing on others' needs. This helps Twos experience a more subtle and acceptable version: pride in their sacrificial love. It is subtle and acceptable because Type Twos settle for being nice in their world: service, helping, other-focused acts, giving of themselves, etc. This results in Twos receiving flattery for being so sacrificial, kind, and thoughtful. These small doses of flattery can confuse the altruism of twos, and feed their subtle pride. Twos' acts of helping are small attempts at giving love to try to satisfy the pursuit of unconditional love.

Type Three ("The Achiever")–Type Threes want worth but settle for image.

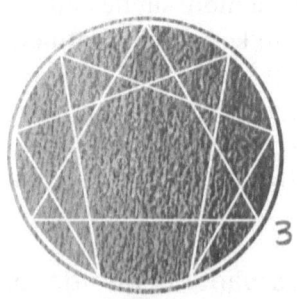

Type Threes are often labeled as "achievers." While this describes common behaviors of Threes, it doesn't capture what Threes are truly after. Threes, at their core, want worth and value. They want to be worthy, and they want the world to be marked by the inherent value of all. But when confronted with a world that doesn't always value the good, the right, and the beautiful, it feels threatening. They can see need for value everywhere, and they see it most prominently within themselves. This leads Type Threes to feel anxious about life, and that stress manifests as shame. But because of their sensitivity to being valued, they hold that shame down whenever possible. Shame then takes on a more subtle and acceptable version: image-crafting to impress and prove their worth. In order to keep the need for worth in check, Type Threes settle for the image(s) they create in their world: accomplished, polished, goal-oriented, and determined. This results in Threes receiving accolades and compliments for being so driven, focused, and successful. These small doses of recognition can confuse the inherent value and worth of Threes, and feed their sense of vanity. The Three's ability to get-things-done are small attempts at seeking the validation we all need.

Type Four ("The Individualist")–Type Fours want belonging but settle for longing.

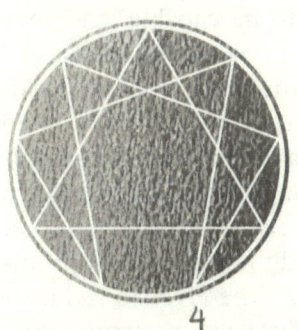

Type Fours are often labeled as "individualists." While this describes some expressions of Fours, it doesn't capture what Fours are truly after. Fours, at their core, want belonging and connection. They want to belong, and they want the world to be marked by connection. But when confronted with a world that doesn't always make space for all as they are, it feels threatening. They can see need for belonging and connection everywhere, and they see it most prominently within themselves. This leads Type Fours to feel anxious about life, and that stress manifests as a particular type of shame: deficiency. Because of their sensitivity to being truly known and accepted, deficiency takes on a more subtle and acceptable version: deep and extraordinary longing for connection. In order to keep the longing in check, Type Fours settle for secondary longings they conjure in their world: the extraordinary, the creative, and the unique. This results in Fours shunning the ordinary and mundane in search of re-establishing depth and connection.

These small doses of uniqueness can confuse the inherent belonging of Fours, and feed their sense of deficiency or inadequacy. Fours' attunement toward being misunderstood drives this pursuit of the unique.

Type Five ("The Investigator")—Type Fives want competency but settle for knowledge.

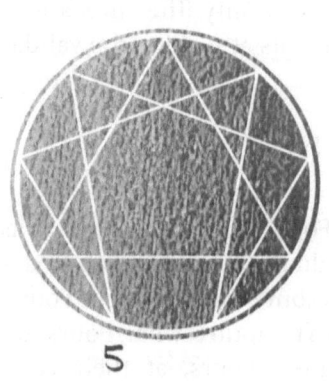

Type Fives are often labeled as "investigators." While this describes some common expressions of Fives, it doesn't capture what Fives are truly after. Fives, at their core, want competency and sufficiency. They want to be capable, and they want the world to be marked by sufficiency of understanding. But when confronted with a world that doesn't always makes sense, or in which they don't feel prepared, it feels threatening. They can see need for competency everywhere, and they see it most prominently within themselves. This leads Type Fives to feel anxious about life, and that stress manifests as a particular type of fear: being useless and empty. Because of their sensitivity to competency, this fear of scarcity takes on a more subtle and acceptable version: depth of knowledge and insatiable curiosity about complex things. In order to keep the need for competency in check, Type Fives settle for the knowledge they acquire in their world: deep dives on complex topics, ideas, or hobbies. This results in Fives' allergies to superficiality, small-talk, and high-energy social engagement. This pursuit of knowledge can cause Fives to withdraw to their safe places to study or tinker, which can further isolate and feed their fear of being useless or incompetent.

Type Six ("The Loyalist")—Type Sixes want loyalty but settle for safety.

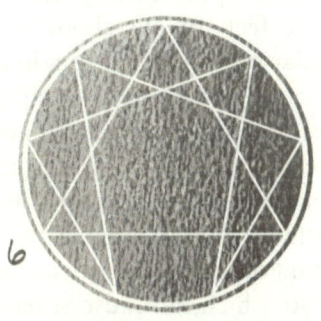

Type Sixes are often labeled as "loyalists." Unlike many other types, this nickname accurately captures what Sixes are truly after. Sixes, at their core, want loyalty. They want to be loyal and supported, and they want the world to be marked by fidelity to one another. But when confronted with a world that isn't always loyal, it feels threatening. They can see need for security everywhere, and they see it most prominently within themselves. This leads Type Sixes to doubt their intuition and feel anxious about life, and that stress manifests as a particular type of fear: being in an unfaithful environment. Because of their need to cope, this fear of infidelity takes on a more subtle and acceptable version: ensuring one's surroundings are safe and secure. In order to keep the need for loyalty in check, Type Sixes settle for the safety they can acquire in their world. This pursuit of safety can cause Sixes to threat-forecast wherever they go, which can further isolate themselves from others and feed their fear of disloyalty.

Type Seven ("The Enthusiast")—Type Sevens want contentment but settle for excitement.

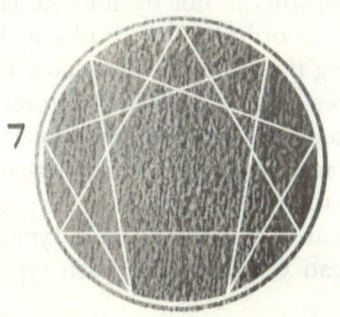

Type Sevens are often labeled as "enthusiasts." While this describes some common expressions of Sevens, it doesn't capture what Sevens are truly after. Sevens, at their core, want contentment. They want to be content, and they want the world to be marked by contentment.

But when confronted with a world that isn't always satisfactory, it feels threatening. They can see need for satisfaction and contentment everywhere, and they see it most prominently within themselves. This leads Type Sevens to feel anxious about life, and that stress manifests as a particular type of fear: being in a painful or deprived environment. Because of their need to cope, this fear of pain or deprivation takes on a more subtle and acceptable version: planning[3] for the next adventure or immersing themselves in another story. In order to keep the need for contentment in check, Type Sevens settle for the excitement they can manifest in their world. This pursuit of excitement can cause Sevens to hyper-plan wherever they go, which can cause Sevens to overlook the goodness of the ordinary and mundane.

Barriers to Discernment

Discernment is the gift and practice of living our lives from a deep sense of vocation, with wisdom, in the fullness of time.

In the Introduction, I argued that our ability to discern our lives well is diminished by lying to ourselves, being overwhelmed, and neglecting to listen. But underneath is another layer of resistance, a marshland of the soul that further impedes. To discern well, we must enter these murky and shadowy places and identify these impediments. More difficult to recognize, these impediments' ability to remain in the shadows makes them more powerful.

Notice how I began the type descriptions above with Type Eight and ended with Type Seven. This is not by mistake (I promise I know how to count). This ordering is a traditional and common approach to exploring the enneagram, because it groups the nine types into the three triads known as the three "centers" of intelligence available to us. We'll explore the centers in depth in Chapter Three, but for now it's helpful to know that types Eight, Nine, and One form the Gut Center Triad, types Two, Three, and Four form the Heart Center Triad, and Types Five, Six, and Seven form the Head Center Triad. Each type tends to lead from their center.

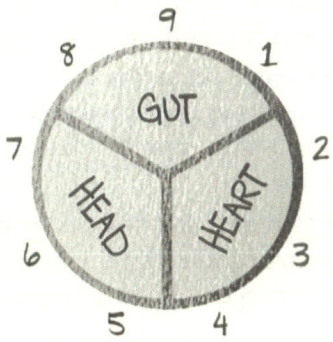

With this in mind, take another look at the descriptions I provide above of the nine types. Look specifically for a word common to the three types in each center.

With this second read, you'll notice three words tend to lift from the pages: anger, shame, and fear. These are the triads' responses to anxiety. We've all been angry. We've all felt shame. We've all been afraid. Any time we experience these emotions, our chances of making poor decisions increase. Our anger blinds. Our shame smothers. Our fear freezes us in our tracks.

Granted, there are healthy expressions of each of these emotions. Righteous anger is a healthy response to injustice or oppression. Shame can give way to remorse and play a healthy role in response to our own wrong and foolish behavior. Many fears are rational and legitimate as a response to real danger.

And it's important to highlight that emotions are vital to our lives. In this book we'll explore how emotions are a form of intelligence. They are a critical component to our wisdom formation. The temptation when we notice how certain emotions impede our discernment is to dismiss them, flee from them, or repress them. Any form of rejecting emotion will lead to poor discernment.

In our adapted states, anger, shame, and fear can result in negative, unhealthy consequences. The enneagram helps us see how each center of intelligence suffers from one of these impeding emotions in a more pronounced way.

- **The Gut Center Triad** types all suffer from anger—a state of displeasure, annoyance or hostility.
- **The Heart Center Triad** types all suffer from shame—a state of painful negative thoughts about oneself, humiliation or distress caused by the experience of being wrong or foolish.
- **The Head Center Triad** types all suffer from fear—an unpleasant state caused by the belief that someone or something is dangerous, likely to cause pain, or a threat.

When we are disconnected from an authentic sense of self, each type slams into a powerful impeding emotion, one they share in common with the other two types in their center. Riso and Hudson refer to this as each center's *dominant* emotion. The enneagram invites us into further exploration of our dominant impeding emotion and its excessive qualities as evidenced in our dominant type. This is the emotion that tends to surface most often to the point that we are nearly fixated on it. And that fixation can bring discernment to a screeching halt.

In the settling statements and descriptions you can see how each type tries to control this dominant emotion in some unhealthy ways. The "settling" for less than what they really want is a sort of compromise. Each type makes an internal deal: "If I settle for ___, it'll keep the dominant emotion (anger, shame, or fear) in check."

This process of controlling the dominant emotion thwarts our discernment in tragic ways.

How Anger Impedes Discernment

When angry, our thoughts become hyper focused on that which caused the anger. Our ability to consider just about anything else wanes, as the brain shunts blood away from itself to our muscles, preparing us for a fight. Our brain's cognitive efficiency (the ability to think clearly and quickly) decreases, and our anxiety increases. The overall effect is that our thinking gets simplified, impeding our ability to slow down, reflect, and engage the complexity of discernment.

In addition, when our bodies are angry we're prone to headaches, migraines, chest pains, or other physical ailments. When our bodies ache, it's difficult to think about anything else. It's a challenge to engage in complex thinking or sustained contemplation when your head is pounding.

Our anger often leads to projecting a false confidence that attempts to minimize risk and increase control. Think of the way many animals strut to appear larger and more menacing. The result is often impulsive behavior causing us to make more mistakes. The humility required of discernment is tossed aside. Our anger can damage relationships, cutting ourselves off from those who could potentially be most helpful in our discernment.

In the Gut Center Triad, Types Eight, Nine, and One are prone to anger in unique ways that impede their ability to discern.

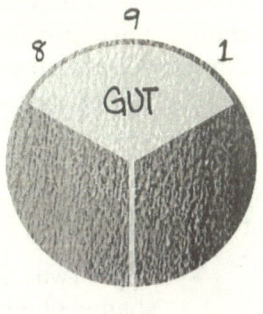

- Type Eights suffer from anger when they sense a lack of protection. They tend to express their anger outwardly, when they anticipate vulnerability or weakness in their world. This type of anger is easy to see as it is often unfiltered. For Eights, it's an efficient way to plow through difficulty or confusion.
- Type Nines suffer from anger at disruption. They tend to resort to a sort of self-forgetting to deny their anger, especially when their environment causes them to remember other disruptive contexts. This denial of anger often seeps out as passive aggression and stubbornness.
- Type Ones suffer from anger at a lack of goodness or rightness. They tend to internalize their anger, shifting its focus to themselves in the form of self-criticism, especially when they experience their world in ways that

lack goodness or rightness. This exposes their own limits and shortcomings and anger can only stay suppressed for so long until it leaks out as resentment.

How Shame Impedes Discernment

Anger smolders until it erupts. Shame comes at us differently. When shame creeps in, it can feel suffocating. When we feel shame, our brains will act to avert any sort of risk, because the possibility of failure reinforces the shame. Our discernment becomes truncated to that which feels safest. Shame has a way of convincing us that we don't deserve any rewards that may come when we risk, so why bother risking at all. Along the way, our self-esteem plummets.

When the body experiences shame, it powers down. Shame has a way of dragging us down like we're sinking in our own quicksand. Momentum wanes, as does the motivation to act out of a sense of discernment. Shame also has a fog-like quality, impeding our vision to see anything but our own shortcomings.

The result is isolation, where we avoid others out of worry about being exposed. In isolation, we're prone to relapse into the same cycles of unhealthy behaviors, which reinforces the shame we loathe. It's a tragic cycle that drains generative discerning energy redirecting it at our own self-loathing.

In the Heart Center Triad, Types Two, Three, and Four are prone to shame in unique ways that impede their ability to discern.

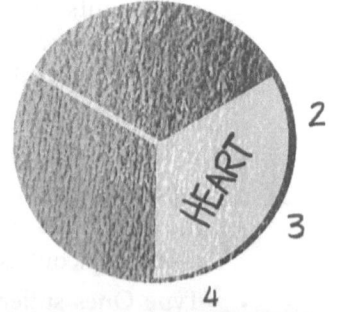

- Type Twos suffer from the shame of being unlovable. They tend to turn their shame into serving and helping others to compensate for the perception of being unloved. This focus on the experience of being loved (or unloved) brings an other-focus. Their shame convinces them that their needs are not worth fulfilling, but others' needs are.

- Type Threes suffer from the shame of being without worth or value. They tend to accomplish and achieve to ward off their anticipation of shame. Their shame tells them that without their abilities to get things done, and look good doing it, they have no worth in their world. This causes Threes to craft personas that they feel are compelling to those around them in order to manufacture a sense of worth.
- Type Fours suffer from the shame of not belonging to something greater than themselves. They tend to channel their shame into longing for what is real and significant. This is often a response to painful memories of not belonging, encouraging Fours to withdraw as a defense. Their shame prods them to search for depth and significance in longing without belonging internally, and re-emerge into their world as one unique: an image that is simultaneously different and yet compelling.

How Fear Impedes Discernment

When we experience fear, our brain short-circuits pathways of rational thinking, reacting more from the amygdala in a survival mode. This process plays tricks with our memory, breeding uncertainty. The uncertainty can be overwhelming, causing us to freeze in our tracks.

When the body is in a state of fear, breathing quickens, the heart races, and muscles tighten in a panic state. The body is not built for sustained fear states, inevitably leading to fatigue and exhaustion, both of which work against the discernment process.

Succumbing to fear over time results in patterns of irrational behavior and/or learned helplessness. When we believe we're in a survival state, we do whatever it takes to survive in the present moment. If fear cripples us, we freeze in a state in which we can't help ourselves. In either situation, the wisdom to discern seems distant.

In the Head Center Triad, Types Five, Six, and Seven are prone to fear in unique ways that impede their ability to discern.

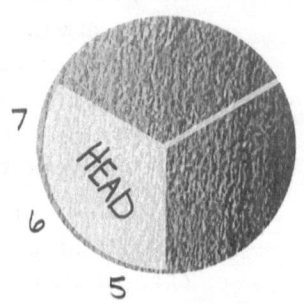

- Type Fives suffer from the fear of being incompetent and insufficient. They can clearly remember times of being without what they deem critical knowledge or information, and they don't want to relive them. This fear drives them to withdraw to study and compile a competency that they feel will protect them when they reemerge in their world.

- Type Sixes suffer from a fear of being without loyalty or support. They tend to experience a lack of security in their environment, which causes them to doubt the support and safety around them. Sixes often want to resolve their perceived threats before they can relax and move ahead. They struggle to trust their own intuition, often looking for assurance from others.

- Type Sevens suffer from a fear of being deprived. They have a sensitivity toward depletion: when excitement, resources, and intrigue will run out. Their fear of being in a state of lack compels them to anticipate how to escape it and move on. This causes them to have one eye on their current environment and one eye on where to go next to maintain a level of contentment.

Anger. Shame. Fear. Their ability to thwart the gift and practice of discernment is pervasive and persistent. But this isn't the end of the story. The more familiar we become with our obstacles, the less ominously they loom over us. When we can name that which is in our way, it doesn't loom over us so ominously. When we can raise our awareness of the unique ways in which our dominant emotion impedes our discernment, its power can diminish. The temptation is to find a way around our anger, around our fear, and around our shame. But avoidance rarely works. We must journey through. When we do, our experiences with anger, shame, and fear can transform from impediments to invitations. These invitations beckon us to the landscape of the Holy.[4] They provide opportunities to listen and decide if the voices of anger, shame, and fear should be the loudest. When we sort through our dominant emotion's voice, we clear the way to hear another Voice. This is God, the Divine Voice of Love, which calls us to authentic identity, purpose, and direction.

Notes

[1] For a brief history of the enneagram, check out a piece written by Mike Morrell and John Luckovich in my friend Dr. Jerome D. Lubbe's beautiful and innovative work, *Whole Identity: A Brain-Based Enneagram Model for (W)holistic Human Thriving, Volume 1*, (Atlanta: Thrive Neuro Theology, 2019), p. 15-17. For a more thorough take, check out Fatima Fernandez Christlieb's *Where (On Earth) Did the Enneagram Come From?* (Fatima Editores, 2016).

[2] See the work of Nicholas Carr, *The Shallows: What the Internet is Doing to Our Brains* (New York: W.W. Norton & Co, 2011).

[3] A word on the "planning" of the Type Seven is needed, as it is often misunderstood by other types. Everyone plans, but the difference with Sevens is that they often plan in the middle of something that they've already planned. Think of planning the next vacation while presently on vacation.

[4] K.J. Ramsey gave me this landscape imagery. It's explored more deeply in her book. See K.J. Ramsey, *This Too Shall Last: Finding Grace When Suffering Lingers* (Grand Rapids: Zondervan, 2020).

CHAPTER TWO

The Vocation Triad: Identity, Purpose, and Direction

> *"We must make the choices that enable us to fulfill the deepest capacities of our real selves."*
> —Thomas Merton

Every step we take is a journey into the unknown. And in between the present moment and the one to come is a space. It's a space of transition, from the now to the next.

At times it's a space pregnant with possibility, where imagination, hope, expectation, all dwell. Not knowing what's next can be exciting. The anticipation can be palpable, fueled by the energy of creativity.

At times it's a space of great confusion, pain, and suffering. Not knowing what's next is often excruciating. The anxiety can be crippling, fueled by the energy of fear. Dare we dream and hope for good things?

Where we are right now is familiar ground. The next step is uncharted territory.

This is liminal space. The word "liminal" comes from the Latin word "limen," which means *threshold*—the sill of a door that marks the transition from one space to another. Many cultures hold special significance for thresholds and pass down customs to bring good luck or ward off bad luck.

Our lives contain many liminal spaces, thresholds from what is quickly becoming old to what is quickly becoming new. The liminal space from the lived to the unlived is sacred ground. Father Richard Rohr refers to liminal space as "God's waiting room."[1]

In God's waiting room, where we don't know what's next, we wait expectantly. In this liminal space, we find the expanse of vocation.

Modern expressions of vocation are unfortunately truncated to one's "job." That's not what I mean. The ancient theological concept of vocation existed long before the age of modern work. It derives from the Latin root *vocare*, which means "to call." Its scope is much broader and deeper. When we talk about calling, we are talking about vocation.[2]

It's a simple, yet profound idea. In the liminal spaces of our lives, where we wonder what's next, a call comes to us from the Divine.[3]

Nearly every religious tradition includes stories of a divinity calling to humanity. Most sacred texts provide dramatic tales of supernatural calls: a bush that burns without being consumed, angelic appearances, donkeys who talk, pillars of fire, golden plates unearthed, etc.

I have to be honest: None of those things have ever happened to me. I've had experiences I can't explain, but nothing so dramatic. Spiritual inspiration in my life has been far more in the realm of faint whispers of guidance, of subtle glints and glimmers. Some drama would make things easier. A bolt of lightning would get my attention.

This is the challenge of vocation: *attention*. Distracted by the enormity of it all, it's tough to pay attention to the Divine, others, and self in the present. Our confusion, anxiety, and worry about what's ahead can max our cognitive load.

But when we pay attention, the whispers of inspiration compel us to widen our eyes, perk our ears, set our jaw, and cross the threshold. It's easier said than done.

For if God calls, what's the Divine saying? And, how are we to respond? Those are hefty questions, loaded with all sorts of baggage.

Such hefty questions emerge in all sorts of important thresholds. We're often faced with decisions that have no simple answer:

- How should I continue my education?
- What should I study?
- Where should I live?
- Whom should I marry?
- Or, should I marry at all?
- What's my ideal career path?
- Do I want to become a parent?

When faced with such important questions, a common response for the religious and non-religious alike is to look to a higher authority (God), to help us make sense of the options before us, or perhaps, provide some validation for what we choose. It's been said that there are no atheists in foxholes.[4] When we feel stuck in indecision, we find ourselves in an existential foxhole.

This isn't all bad. To explore a calling is a noble thing. It's a means of placing one's life in a larger picture. Also, a calling assumes a Caller. That's also a good thing. To bring calling into our discernment means acknowledging our search for wisdom's source in making decisions.

To hear and respond to a sense of calling beckons us to cross the threshold into our unlived lives. How does this work? To be honest, much of what occurs in liminal space is spiritual and mystical, difficult to describe in words. It's more alchemic than formulaic. Our lives are marked by both clarity and confusion when it comes to our thresholds. Each of us can remember times in which the way forward was crystal clear. In my own life, the decisions to marry my wife was one such "crystal clear" threshold. We can also recall moments in which we had no idea what to do next. I've faced numerous career-related decisions that felt like a coin-flip was my only help. The temptation is to try to find a shortcut—a way to get from here to there (whatever there we hope and dream) as quickly as possible. We want to jump from our current place to a destination.

A definition is helpful to begin to wrap our minds, hearts, and bodies around vocation. I consider vocation to be ***receiving the Divine Call of identity, purpose, and direction***.

A few aspects of this definition are worth highlighting. First, vocation is a gift more than it is a goal. Western culture has exalted the driven life, which often compels us to set goals ahead and then work toward them. This isn't necessarily wrong. Goal setting can be healthy. But importing it into the realm of vocation can distort the beautiful gift of the Divine Call. Palmer perhaps says it best when he describes vocation "not as a goal to be achieved but as a gift to be received. Discovering vocation does not mean scrambling toward some prize just beyond my reach but accepting the treasure of true self I already possess."[5] Receiving the gift is a lifelong process. There very well may be important destinations along the way, but they are cairns in the expanse of vocation.

Second, this definition surveys the expanse of vocation, which includes three sacred territories: identity, purpose, and direction. To discern our lives well, we can't bypass identity, purpose, and direction. Calling isn't something we simply descend upon. We make this road by walking it. The journey to a wild and precious life emerges from the Divine Call to traverse these territories.

In the expanse of Vocation Triad, we encounter the first three key questions of discernment:

- Who am I?—This is the question of identity.
- Why am I here?—This is the question of purpose.
- Where am I going?—This is the question of direction.

And in this space, these beautiful and brave questions emerge. Trace your confusion, frustration, and pain…you'll eventually get to one of these questions.

Navigating the big questions is not easy. These three territories don't always provide specific answers when crossing life's thresholds. But they provide us with something better: the confidence to cross any threshold with authenticity and integrity.

Let's explore each of these territories in turn, and how the Enneagram of Discernment provides insight.

The First Territory: Identity

Our Caricatures

Not too long ago I was on vacation with my family and there was a street artist offering to draw caricature portraits. I'm sure you've seen them: cartoonish likenesses of a person with exaggerated features. I think there's a reason they play well on streets and boardwalks the world over: in such drawings we see a comical version of ourselves. They're fun and funny, an impulsive artifact from the day.

Caricature artists can produce a portrait for you in mere minutes, which is astonishing. Their ability to produce a mimicked version of a person fascinates the passerby. There's also a deeper truth to it. The word, which derives from the Italian language, originally meant "loaded portrait." Caricatures are simultaneously loaded with simplifications and exaggerations.

It's an art with a hustle, which I can respect. But it's also something we've all been doing to ourselves for the entirety of our lives. Psychologists, theologians, and spiritual directors have long talked about the idea of the "false self" (in contrast with the "true self"). Different teachers have different ways of talking about the false and true selves, but all agree that, as children, we all develop a sense of self that helps us survive and navigate our worlds. Let me be clear that this is not a bad thing. Survival and coping are essential. But we, like the caricaturists, find ways to simplify and exaggerate who we are. Over time, we become a version of ourselves that we can recognize, but isn't truly who we are.

Gradually, we begin to rely too heavily on an ego that we've developed. Again, recall Nouwen's three lies of identity:

- I am what I have.
- I am what I do.
- I am what others say about me.

Living the lies over time develops a dependence on a false self that seeks to live our lives out of our own strength, disconnected from God. Consider how each lie falls into this trap:

- I am defined by the wealth I possess. Therefore, I must continue to accumulate more money and possessions in order to understand who I am.
- I am defined by the work that I do. Therefore, I must continue to work harder and move up the "ladder" in order to understand who I am.
- I am defined by how other's perceive me. Therefore, I must find ways to please and impress those around me in order to understand who I am.

Read over the above again. Notice the perpetual striving required. Notice how identity is defined by external forces. This is the false self. Albert Haase, in his book, *Coming Home to Your True Self*, expands this idea, providing ten "Empty P's of the False Self:" pleasure, praise, power, prestige, position, popularity, people, productivity, possessions, perfection.[6]

Our ability to develop our identity in unhealthy places abounds. Enneagram author and teacher Marylin Vancil describes this development in a helpful way. She refers to this as the "adapted self," the self we believe we must be in order to survive and have our needs met.[7]

This false/adapted self is the result of an over-identification with our ego. Granted, part of being human is having an ego. In fact, the ego is responsible for some important functions of our overall self. Beware the teachers who claim to help you eradicate your ego, allowing you to simply live from "essence." The goal is not to have our ego disappear. To have an ego is not a problem. To have an ego is to be human.

The problem is over-identifying with our ego, letting it run our lives. This is *egocentricity*. David Benner describes it this way: "it (the ego) cannot fulfill the role it is uniquely equipped to fill while it functions as chief executive officer."[8] In other words, our ego must be put in its proper place, letting our authentic self lead the way.

Authentic Self

You can probably see where I'm going. A helpful way to understand the adapted self is the enneagram types. My friend Seth Abram has a helpful take. He considers this false/adapted self a part of us that "lacks trust in being created in the image of the Divine."[9] The absence of trust in one's own authentic identity is a powerful motivator to place trust in other things, hoping they will help us understand who we are. Coupled with a lifetime of results in which our adapted self has worked fairly well for us, discovering a different way of being is no small task.

And the current go-to methods of self-improvement aren't all that helpful. They're full of willfulness (more on this later) and striving. The path to a more authentic self isn't a hot topic in the self-help space. Peeling back the adapted self to a more authentic way of living takes great time and care. We relax into it more than we go get it. We receive it as a gift more than we create it.[10] And that authentic self, for every person, regardless of enneagram type, is this:

You are a beloved self-in-God, made in the image of the Divine.

The word *beloved* has been reduced to mere sentimentality, but let's look at the original meaning. The prefix "be" conveys ideas such as "completely covered," and "encompassing." Your authentic self is one who is completely covered and encompassed in love. In this way, your authentic self has nothing to do with your behavior. It has everything to do with love.

This love is also generative. We are created in the *Imago Dei*, as an imprint of the Divine. Consider David Benner's explanation:

> …our being is grounded in God's love. The generative love of God was our origin. The embracing love of God sustains…Love is our identity…Created from love, of love and for love, our existence makes no sense apart from Divine love.[11]

This is the beautiful irony of identity. We are prone to craft our own imprints to survive and thrive in our world. But our authentic identity is an imprint of a different sort, one that authenticates instead of imitates.

By excavating our way through the layers of adapted self that we've confused with identity, we reach the core of who we are: love in the *Imago Dei*.[12] Love doesn't simplify to reduce. Love doesn't exaggerate to compensate. Love doesn't divide. Love doesn't diminish. Love has a way of re-joining, re-conciling, re-deeming, and re-membering. In word, love is the way of wholeness.

And here we find the starkness of contrast between the adapted self and the authentic self. One is a caricature self with clever features. The other is a core self defined by wholeness.

Thomas Kelly, the Quaker mystic, calls this authentic self the "Divine Center," a holy place within us with a speaking Voice.[13] Many traditions call this Spirit. In the Christian tradition, St. John refers to the Spirit using the Greek word "*paraclete*," which translates as "helper," "advocate," or "counselor." What is more essential to discernment than a loving advocate/helper/counselor?

Now we've rounded an important circle: We too often look for a voice "out there" to guide us, when very often the voice we need to listen to is within. External voices and influences can certainly help, but we should never rely upon them at the expense of the Divine within. From this place of Divine Love we can hear guidance without pretense, insight without agenda, and encouragement without disclaimers. In our authentic self, union with God is available. This Divine Love helps us distinguish from the other inner voices (inner critics) that seek to sabotage us: chiefly anger, shame, and fear.

From Adapted Self → Authentic Self

To authentically live from this place is not easy. It requires much of us in areas we've learned to ignore. This work of excavation requires seven steps.

First, we must be more *aware* of our adapted self. It starts with an awareness of the ways in which we have learned to survive and cope, even when it has produced some great results.

Second, we must *acknowledge* the Divine Voice who calls us "beloved." This union with God that is available to us is a beautiful relationship defined by love that frames all relationships. The question *Who am I?* leads us to another question: *Whose am I?*. Our selfhood resides in the realm of relationships. To receive this call as a gift requires us to acknowledge a Giver, and be grateful for the gift. Benner writes, "Nothing is more important, for if we find our true self we find God, and if we find God, we find our most authentic self."[14]

Third, we must *relinquish* our adapted self. Over many years we've developed strong attachments to our adapted self. It's a place of some comfort and familiarity. To let it go can be scary. I've often heard that spirituality is really the art of letting go. When it comes to identity, we must begin to loosen our grip on our caricatured notions of self in order to receive the gift of identity.

Fourth, we must approach the path with *humility*. The journey to the authentic self is rarely triumphant. It's more of a humble quest in which we confront ways in which we've simplified and exaggerated ourselves in unhealthy ways. Think of a time in which you were humbled. Such instances have a way of bringing us back down to earth. It can hurt, but it can also ground us. The firmness of the ground provides a measure of safety and firmness upon which to walk.[15]

Fifth, we must *befriend* ourselves. Palmer reminds us that "true self is true friend."[16] If we are made in the image and likeness of God, and our identity is that of beloved, we must claim this as our identity and befriend it.

Sixth, we must live from a place of *agency*. The energetic nature of Love cannot be contained. From our identity as beloved we draw loving energy from the Divine Source. This is fertile ground from which to live, and here our sense of being and our sense of doing find congruence. Our activity in the world flows from this place of identity.

Seventh, we must continually do all of the above. I wish I could tell you that this chapter is a one-time ride. With honesty I can tell you that this journey of awareness, acknowledgement, befriending, humility, and surrender is lifelong and comprised of many iterations. But please don't mistake this journey for any other journey that calls you to strive or manufacture. The path from adapted to authentic is a descent. A journey inward and downward through our shadows. In many ways, this is the more difficult path. When Jesus told his disciples that to save their lives they must lose it (Mark 8:34-36), this is what he was talking about. There is a death we must suffer: a death to our over-identification with the ego. We must slay our overreliance of the unhealthy adapted self. Out of this death is resurrection.

Thomas Merton once wrote, "For me to be a saint means to be myself." This is what it means to live from authentic self. While this journey from adaptation to authenticity is available to us all, the places from which we start may differ. This is where enneagram wisdom helps us identify our dominant place of the adapted self (dominant type).

Enneagram Type → Authentic Self

The personality we've developed helps us survive, but it creates problems as it solves others. While it keeps us safe, it also conspires in our own diminishment and division.[17] This is where the enneagram provides a deep well of understanding. When we look at the specific ways in which each enneagram type seeks to present an adapted self to survive in the world, we can begin to find our way back to a more authentic self. We'll explore each types' path to authentic self in Part II of the book, but for now let's consider how each type adapts:[18]

- Type 1: Those dominant in Type One believe they must be right and live up to high ideals to be safe.

- Type 2: Those dominant in Type Two believe they must be "loving" and connected to others to be safe.
- Type 3: Those dominant in Type Three believe they must be successful and impressive to be safe.

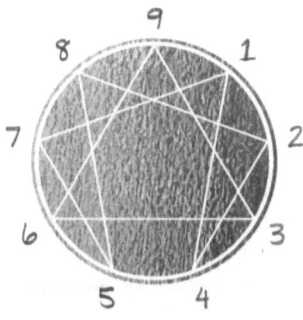

- Type 4: Those dominant in Type Four believe they must be unique and significant to be safe.
- Type 5: Those dominant in Type Five believe they must be competent and at a safe distance from others to be safe.
- Type 6: Those dominant in Type Six believe they must be responsible and secure in their surroundings to be safe.
- Type 7: Those dominant in Type Seven believe they must be free and occupied to be safe.
- Type 8: Those dominant in Type Eight believe they must be powerful and in control to be safe.
- Type 9: Those dominant in Type Nine believe they must be peaceful and easygoing to be safe.

From our dominant type, we begin to see how we each deploy the human instincts of survival to develop an adapted self. In this adaptation, like the caricature, we simplify certain aspects of ourselves and exaggerate others. Our simplifications diminish a full and authentic sense of who we truly are. And our exaggerations further divide ourselves from a sense of wholeness.

This is why, when we take the time to honestly look at the life we're living, we so often see misplaced priorities, disordered and distorted loves, and fragmentation.

But the good news is that this isn't the end of the story. Wholeness and authenticity are within. While the enneagram teaches us that we will lead with our dominant type for the rest of our lives, its dominance in this adapted state can experience its own diminishment. We can put the ego in its proper place. When we reclaim a sense of authentic self, the simplicities and exaggerations of the adapted self soften their grip. This is the path to authenticity, to a sense of self defined not by external forces but from a deeper Source.

The path to authenticity requires a great *unknowing*, where we unlearn some messages that bolster the adapted self, so that we can begin to know what it means to live from the authentic self.

Look again at the list above, where I provide a statement for how each enneagram type adapts. If you know your dominant type, consider this: What if you lived as if your adaptation statement wasn't true?

It would require some "unknowing." For my dominant Type Three, I would have to unknow my patterns and habits that reinforce the idea that my safety and survival hinges upon my ability to be successful and impress others. For many types, that's not a big deal. For a Type Three, it's the tallest mountain to climb.

This process of unknowing begins with the acknowledgment of what needs to be challenged.

Riso and Hudson provide two lists of childhood messages that highlight what I believe to be the unknowing work for each type. First let's consider the "Unconscious Childhood Messages" for each type. These are the messages we believed to be true as children, which catalyze the development of the dominant enneagram types:

Unconscious Childhood Messages:[19]

Type 1 - "It's not okay to make mistakes."

Type 2 - "It's not okay to have your own needs."

Type 3 - "It's not okay to have your own feelings and identity."

Type 4 - "It's not okay to be too functional or too happy."

Type 5 - "It's not okay to be comfortable in the world."

The Vocation Triad: Identity, Purpose, and Direction

Type 6 - "It's not okay to trust yourself."

Type 7 - "It's not okay to depend on anyone for anything."

Type 8 - "It's not okay to be vulnerable or to trust anyone."

Type 9 - "It's not okay to assert yourself."

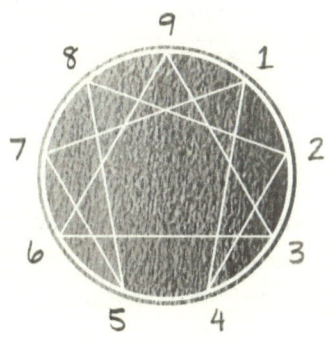

Next compare this with Riso and Hudson's other list of childhood messages, the "Lost Childhood Messages." Here we see that somewhere along the way we lost sight of these truths and instead starting living from a place of being "not okay":

Lost Childhood Messages:[20]

Type 1 - "You are good."

Type 2 - "You are wanted."

Type 3 - "You are loved for yourself."

Type 4 - "You are seen for who you are."

Type 5 - "Your needs are not a problem."

Type 6 - "You are safe."

Type 7 - "You will be taken care of."

Type 8 - "You will not be betrayed."

Type 9 - "Your presence matters."

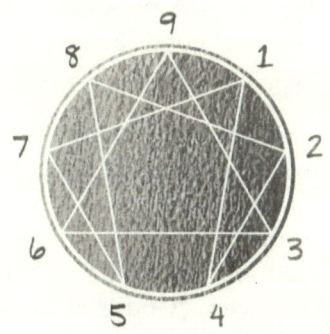

Let's combine the two lists to begin to explore the way of unknowing for each type. We must unknow the first message to embrace what was once lost.

Unconscious Childhood Messages → Lost Childhood Messages

Type 1 - "It's not okay to make mistakes." → "You are good."

Type 2 - "It's not okay to have your own needs." → "You are wanted."

Type 3 - "It's not okay to have your own feelings and identity." → "You are loved for yourself."

Type 4 - "It's not okay to be too functional or too happy." → "You are seen for who you are."

Type 5 - "It's not okay to be comfortable in the world." → "Your needs are not a problem."

Type 6 - "It's not okay to trust yourself." → "You are safe."

Type 7 - "It's not okay to depend on anyone for anything." → "You will be taken care of."

Type 8 - "It's not okay to be vulnerable or to trust anyone." → "You will not be betrayed."

Type 9 - "It's not okay to assert yourself." → "Your presence matters."

For many, the chasm between your unconscious childhood message and lost childhood message seems enormous. But with awareness and intention, each dominant type can navigate the territory of identity. Our dominant type is the trailhead to a sacred journey to the authentic self as beloved. Meister Eckhart once said, "God is at home. It is we who have gone out for a walk."[21] To live our lives with discernment, we must first go home. From there we receive the gift of our authentic purpose.

The Second Territory: Purpose

Olympic athletes are well known for their one pure and clear purpose: to get the gold medal. Every summer and winter Olympic games of my childhood were marked with televised biographical stories of athletes who sacrificed many things in the pursuit of Olympic glory. I was an aspiring athlete myself as a child, so I got it. But one athlete's story complicated things for me: Eric Liddell. Liddell was a Scottish Olympic Gold medalist whose story is recounted in the movie *Chariots of Fire*. Perhaps the most famous quote from the film subverted my simplistic idea of purpose. "I believe that God made me for a purpose. . . and when I run, I feel his pleasure. . .to win is to honor him."[22] Liddell's story raised more questions within me than answers: *Why did I want to win? Why did I want to be first?* Purpose, I eventually learned, is a complex thing. Even among the world's elite athletes, purposes can differ. The "why" behind something has many layers.

Remember that when we embark on the journey from the adapted to authentic self, we eventually discover a new energy of agency. This agency activates our journey through vocation's second territory: purpose.

It is in this territory we engage the second question of the Vocation Triad: *Why am I here?*

This territory is also fraught with dangers. In our striving and our ambition, we are tempted to cast purpose as a motivating force that drives us toward a goal. It's good to have goals. But pursuing a goal must come from a deeper place. If we only tend to the shallower purposes in life, we live from a place of willfulness. It's a forced set of "yeses" and "nos" that come from an external place. It's conjured and mustered. Parker Palmer goes so far to consider willfulness as an act of violence toward the self.[23] Our response to the Divine Call isn't one of willfulness but willingness. Willfulness is oppositional. Willingness is consensual.[24] To live in agreement with the Divine Call sets a purpose that is deeper than our goals and ambitions and flows directly from our identity as the beloved self-in-God.

An identity doesn't exist in a vacuum. It's a lived experience in homes, schools, neighborhoods, families, congregations and relationships. This is where purpose resides, in the **intention** of our identity. Once we discover our authentic self, how do we live from it?

This is the central *why* of vocation, the intent of our identity. It's here that I believe another ancient theological concept is truly helpful.

Shalom is an ancient Hebrew concept found throughout the Jewish *Tanakh* (to the Christians, the Old Testament). It's commonly translated as "peace" in English, which is a travesty. A more proper translation of *shalom* is "flourishing." In the ancient Hebrew wisdom tradition, *shalom* means flourishing in the expanse of life. It's a call to live a life in pursuit of flourishing in one's relationships with God, self, others, and creation. So, when we talk about purpose in our vocation, we're talking about a process of living in healthy trajectories of shalom in the many dimensions of our lives.

It's a beautiful notion: to live as the beloved self-in-God is to be about the belovedness of others. The Divine Love is self-giving rather than self-serving. It flows from God to our self-in-God and to other selves-in-God through our relationships. When we live from a place of authentic identity in the *Imago Dei*, our self also gives from this same Source. This allows us to consent to right relationships with God, self, others, and creation.

Shalom thus provides an even greater vision of wholeness. The journey of discovering the *Imago Dei*, moving from adapted self to authentic self heals us from our egocentricity, unifying our self with God. This is an internal wholeness. Shalom helps us seek flourishing wholeness around us. It aligns our self-in-God with others in generative, reciprocating ways.

When our identity and purpose are aligned, we can name how our dominant enneagram type settles for a life that is less than flourishing. We can also see more clearly the gifts we offer the world, one that acknowledges our *Imago Dei* and seeks to flourish from this identity. Consider this a way of willingness for each type.

Purpose: From Settling → Flourishing

Type 1 – Ones want goodness but settle for order. → Goodness is within. → Pursue flourishing from this inner goodness.

Type 2 – Twos want unconditional love but settle for niceness. → Love is within → Pursue flourishing from this inner love.

Type 3 – Threes want worth but settle for image → Worth is within. → Pursue flourishing from this inner worth.

Type 4 – Fours want belonging but settle for longing → Belonging is within. → Pursue flourishing from this inner belonging.

Type 5 – Fives want competency but settle for knowledge → Competency is within → Pursue flourishing from this inner competency.

Type 6 – Sixes want loyalty but settle for safety → Loyalty is within. → Pursue flourishing from this inner loyalty.

Type 7 – Sevens want contentment but settle for excitement. → Contentment is within. → Pursue flourishing from this inner contentment.

Type 8 – Eights want protection but settle for control. → Protection is within. → Pursue flourishing from this inner protection.

Type 9 – Nines want peace but settle for calm. → Peace is within. → Pursue flourishing from this inner peace.

There's much more to say about willingness of purpose for each type. Part II of the book will explore this more deeply. For all types, a helpful starting place for flourishing relationships is approaching others with the following mantra: *The image of God in me sees the image of God in you.* By stating this in our encounters with others (even if internally), we name and acknowledge the identity of others. This is the beginning of the pursuit of flourishing.

The Third Territory: Direction

We've crossed the first two territories of the Vocation Triad, and now we encounter the third: direction. This territory explores the third question of discernment: *Where am I going?* It's a question about the future, an expressed hope to see where things end. We're all prone to look ahead, squinting our eyes to notice what's in the distance.

This third territory is uniquely challenging. We can't fast forward our lives. Our predictions of the future are often incorrect.

The unforeseen nature of life can cause anxiety. We run into all sorts of things for which we did not prepare.

When we align this third question, *Where am I going?* with the questions of identity and purpose, our direction shifts. Rather than anxiously looking ahead, we discern with depth our present trajectory. And here we encounter another ancient concept: the *fathom*.

The term "fathom" originally meant "outstretched arms." Well before sophisticated marine technology, sailors and mariners would use a sounding line to measure the depths of the water beneath their boats. This ancient nautical tool was brilliantly simple: a thick rope with a weight on the one end. A member of the crew would take a length of rope equivalent to their outstretched arms and then drop it into the water.

This was one fathom. Again: two fathoms. Again: three.

Repeat the process until the weight reaches bottom, and you could comprehend the depths of where you are by the number of fathoms.

Fathom by fathom, sailors could measure the depth of where they were. Over time, "fathom" came to mean the way in which we understand a difficult problem or situation. We take the time to penetrate the surface, and, bit-by-bit, come to a place of comprehension.

This is the Divine Call to discern direction. We comprehend where we are going by considering what we can reach with our arms. Then we do it again. And again. In this is a great mercy. If we attempt to comprehend all that awaits us, we'll be overwhelmed. But fathom by fathom, we make our way.

The direction of vocation is one of depth before distance. With arms outstretched, we discern by seeing beneath the surface of where we are and seeing through with wisdom: we notice complexities and intricacies. We take the necessary time to understand this fathom, and then we measure the next.

Then, from an authentic identity as self-in-God, in the pursuit of flourishing, we take the next right step. Then the next.

Each enneagram type is called to fathom in ways that are congruent with our identity and purpose and uncomfortable to our adapted self. We'll consider them in Part II.

Conclusion

In the many thresholds of our lives, God is calling. The Divine rarely (if ever) provides a formula. This is not the realm of 10 year strategic plans. What God gives in this liminal space are deeper truths: identity, purpose, and direction. These territories of vocation transcend all our plans. This is true vocation: an understanding of who you are, why you are here, and where you are going.

- *Who are you?* A beloved self-in-God.
- *Why are you here?* To pursue flourishing; wholeness in your relationships with God, self, others, and creation.
- *Where are you going?* Fathom, by fathom, you will comprehend the depths of your journey.

Our egocentricism blinds us to these truths, relying on our own willfulness to make our way in the world. But freedom from this "false self" loosens the chains of our anger, shame, and fear, and allows us to take a posture of willingness, where we say "Yes!" to God's call.

Notes

[1] https://cac.org/liminal-space-2016-07-07/.

[2] Since vocation's etymological roots are so similar to that of "calling," I use the two terms synonymously. Therefore, I won't use the common phrase, "vocation and calling" because I think it's redundant.

[3] Admittedly, words fail when describing the transcendent. They are limiting the limitless; attempting to define the indescribable. God, the Divine, Ultimate Reality, Essence, the Universe all carry certain meaning and connotation, attempting to grasp at that which is transcendent and universal. For consistency, I'll be using God and the Divine. I approach my experience in this world from a Christian perspective but am hoping to present this material from a more inclusive "faith positive" perspective.

[4] The origin of this quote is unknown and disputed.

[5] Palmer, *Let Your Life Speak*, p. 10.

[6] Albert Haase, *Coming Home to Your True Self: Leaving the Emptiness of False Attractions* (Downers Grove, IL: InterVarsity Press, 2008).

[7] Marilyn Vancil, *Self to Lose, Self to Find: A Biblical Approach to the 9 Enneagram Types* (Enumclaw, WA: Redemption Press, 2016).

[8] David G. Benner, *Soulful Spirituality: Becoming Fully Alive and Deeply Human* (Grand Rapids: Brazos Press, 2011), p. 64.

[9] Follow Seth's brilliant work on Instagram at @intedgratedenneagram.

[10] Benner's *The Gift of Being Yourself* helped me with this language.

[11] Benner, *The Gift of Being Yourself*, p. 47.

[12] Throughout this book, especially in Part II, I call each enneagram type to return to, discover, or reclaim that which it truly "wants." I often use language such as "inherent worth, peace, value, protection," etc. When I do, I'm referring to this *Imago Dei* within us, the Divine imprint which reflects these characteristic of God.

[13] I found this in Chuck DeGroat's fabulous book *Wholeheartedness: Busyness, Exhaustion, and Healing the Divided Self* (Grand Rapids: Eerdmans Publishing, 2016), p 130-131.

[14] Benner, *The Gift of Being Yourself*, p. 17.

[15] Palmer's *Let Your Life Speak* talks similarly about the benefits of "humiliation."

[16] Palmer, *Let Your Life Speak*, p. 69.

[17] Again, I'm channeling Parker Palmer's work here in *Let Your Life Speak*.

[18] The language here is mine, but informed by some underlying motivations work provided by Don Richard Riso and Russ Hudson.

[19] Don Richard Riso and Russ Hudson, *The Wisdom of the Enneagram: The Complete Guide to Psychological and Spiritual Growth for the Nine Personality Types* (New York: Bantam Press, 1999).

[20] This list is from Riso and Hudson's *The Wisdom of the Enneagram*.

[21] This quote is widely attributed to the German mystic Meister Eckhart. Mentz, George, See Meister Eckhart, *The Complete Mystical Works of Meister Eckhart* (New York: Crossroad Publishing, 2009).

[22] Anderson, Lindsay, Cheryl Campbell, Ian Charleson, Dennis Christopher, Ben Cross, Nigel Davenport, Brad Davis, et al. 2011. *Chariots of Fire*: Warner Home Video.

[23] Palmer, *Let Your Life Speak*, p. 4.

[24] In David Benner's *Desiring God's Will: Aligning Our Hearts with the Heart of God* (Downers Grove, IL: InterVarsity Press, 2015), this is a central concept.

CHAPTER THREE

The Wisdom Triad: Doing, Feeling, Thinking

*"Blessed are those who find wisdom,
those who gain understanding."*
—Proverbs 3:13

"Love is the highest form of intelligence."
—Serge Benhayon[1]

When we consider the many decisions of life, how do we *know* that the decisions we make are the 'right' ones? Questions of identity, purpose, and direction are weighty ones. They often lack the general consensus that accompanies "harder" science such as gravity. I know that if I jump off a cliff I will fall instead of fly. But when it comes to discerning with wisdom, we must honestly confront the question: How do we know what we need to know in order to live a flourishing life?

For philosophers, it's a question of epistemology. For psychologists, it's a question of consciousness. For neuroscientists, it's a question of biology. For sociologists, it's a question of context. For theologians, it's a question of divine inspiration.

To consider how we know what we know can take our thoughts to some strange and confusing places. First, we must consider the process (or pathways) by which we gain insight to take good and healthy steps of progress in our lives. In other words, our experience of knowing matters greatly.

And when it comes to matters of discernment, not all content is created equal. It's tragically ironic in our information-saturated culture; when we can access anything with our smart phones, we are no wiser when it comes to life's most important questions. Information must be perceived, analyzed, filtered, considered, and critiqued. We have more than enough *information* to make decisions. What we often lack is proper understanding, application, and purpose. Consider this:

- Information is purely content
- Knowledge is content understood
- Wisdom is understanding applied for what truly matters

This is what the great twentieth century poet T.S. Eliot was championing in his iconic poem "The Rock":

The endless cycle of idea and action,
Endless invention, endless experiment,
Brings knowledge of motion, but not of stillness;
Knowledge of speech, but not of silence;
Knowledge of words, and ignorance of the Word.
All our knowledge brings us nearer to our ignorance,
All our ignorance brings us nearer to death,
But nearness to death no nearer to God.
Where is the Life we have lost in living?
Where is the wisdom we have lost in knowledge?
Where is the knowledge we have lost in information?[2]

In the Introduction, I argued that INFORMATION < KNOWLEDGE < WISDOM. Eliot's poem corroborates this. To become wise, we must better understand the various ways we can know and better apply them to what truly matters. In this chapter we will explore the ways in which we experience what we know—our perceptions, our analyses, our interpretations, and our responses to the knowledge. As you might guess, the Enneagram of Discernment helps us cultivate wisdom for this journey. We'll first start with an introduction to Divine Love as a way of knowing. Then we'll consider how all humans have three centers of knowing. Then we'll explore how the enneagram helps us make sense of it all.

Love as a Way of Being...and Knowing

At a fundamental level, I think the enneagram can illuminate pathways for us to the God who is Love. And, when we embark on this journey, we experience the most powerful, guiding, and animating force in the universe: Love. Think of Love as a way of knowing that cultivates the wisdom we need to live well.

Contemplative physicist Arthur Zajonc, in an interview with Krista Tippett, argued that "Love allows us gently, respectfully, and intimately to slip in the life of another person . . . In this way, love can become a way of moral knowing that is as reliable as scientific insight."[3] Love fuels our ability to know. This contrasts other understandings of knowing, which seek to rid the process of all emotion to elevate objective reasoning, to let the facts speak for themselves.

Consider the ways in which knowing is portrayed in the Christian Bible. In the New Testament, Jesus of Nazareth, when asked by the religious elite which commandment in the law is greatest, provides a two-part response. First, "Love the Lord your God with all your heart, with all your soul, and with all your mind" (Matt. 22:37, NIV). The original Greek terms used for "heart," "soul," and "mind" are insightful:[4]

- Heart—The Greek word used here is *kardia*. In ancient Greek, the *kardia* is the center of understanding, the fountain and seat of the thoughts, passions, desires, appetites, affections, purposes, and endeavors.
- Soul—The Greek word used here is *psuche*. In ancient Greek, the *psuche* is the vital force which animates the body and shows itself in breathing.

- Mind—The Greek word used here is *dianoia*. The faculty (the ability or power) to understand. This is the center of thinking.

Our minds, our hearts, and our souls are called to love God. In similar fashion, Jesus continues with the second part of his response, "Love your neighbor as yourself" (Matt 22:39). Our minds, our hearts, and our souls are likewise called to love others and ourselves, in the pursuit of flourishing. This *agape* love, or Divine Love, flows from God to creation as a sacrifice, ultimately expressed in Jesus's loving sacrifice on the cross of crucifixion.

Divine Love is pure and sacrificial. Thus, it's not selfish or self-serving. It's self-giving. It's a perfect love in that it is complete. Consider the times in your life where you felt particularly vulnerable, where your wounds or faults were laid bare. The most powerful love from others is when they truly *know* you, warts and all, and yet truly *love* you anyway.

This love is the very essence of God. Read the book of I John in the New Testament, and it's unmistakable. "God is love" (I John 4). Divine Love is who God is. Dr. David Benner wrote, in my opinion, one of the greatest treatises on Divine Love in print. In *Surrender to Love*, he reminds us that "the love of God is the most basic ingredient in the cosmos."[5] And, because God is love, and we are made in God's image, love is more than just a feeling or even an action. In the Vocation Triad (Chapter Two), we explored how love is core to who we are. In the Wisdom Triad, we now consider how love is core to how we know.

Thus, the "point of being human is to learn love."[6] It's to learn to be ourselves in the ways in which God intended. This doesn't solve the mysteries and complexities of calling, but it does give us a deep and rich place to start. We are knowers because we are lovers.

Divine Love that cultivates wisdom saturates the next three questions in the Way of Discernment:

- What am I doing?
- What am I feeling?
- What am I thinking?

Beneath these three "simple" questions are the riches of wisdom, a holistic intelligence that transcends intellect. Jesus's words convey this truth. The philosopher James K.A. Smith puts it this way: "Jesus is a teacher who doesn't just inform our intellect but forms our very loves. He isn't content to simply deposit new ideas into your mind; he is after nothing less than your wants, your loves, your longings."[7] Such "loves" are formed in our whole selves: gut, heart, and head. Divine Love is a *wise* love—one that forms and transforms us.

Thus, our loves and our intelligence are more intertwined than we're often willing to admit. Love and knowledge are in a close relationship in our very being, and they can either work to keep us trapped in our old habits and patterns, or they can cultivate wisdom to discern our path faithfully.

The Three Centers of Knowing

Jesus's call to love God and others employs a three-part framework (heart, soul, mind). Similarly, the enneagram teaches a triad of knowing, commonly referred to as the centers of intelligence: the head, the heart, and the gut (or body).

Most enneagram teachers who work with the centers of intelligence draw from the work of Scottish psychiatrist Dr. Maurice Nicoll who wrote at length on the importance of the three intelligence centers: the head, the heart, and the gut (or, the body).[8] Think of each as a hub of knowing, meaning-making and intelligence. We find explorations of these three centers in many streams of psychology, many ancient spiritual traditions, and more recently, in neuroscience.

We all have a head, a heart, and a gut, but we tend not to use all three as we should. As we discovered in Chapter One, each center suffers a dominant emotion (anger, shame, or fear) that impedes discernment. But it doesn't have to be this way. We are smarter than we think we are. We have three centers to perceive, interpret, and analyze our experience. These three centers provide important ways to love God, love ourselves, and love others well. When considered together, many enneagram teachers refer to these three centers as the triadic self. This triadic intelligence is vitally important in our discernment, starting with our ability to experience God.

When we use them well, in an integrated way, we can see and engage the fullness of our present experience. Many enneagram teachers will refer to the three intelligence centers as a three-legged stool.[9] We need all three legs in order to sit. That's a helpful image, but I'd like to propose another. I think of the intelligence centers as three persons in a beautiful, coordinated dance. Flow. Rhythm. Beauty. Together they create something more complete and beautiful than the sum of their individual efforts.

If we consider the three centers of intelligence as the head, the heart, and the gut, then we can begin to see what each center offers us. Enneagram teachers Kathy Hurley and Theodorre Donson have done some of the best work in this area, which has been more recently developed and expanded by Suzanne Stabile. The head center provides us "thinking intelligence," the heart center provides us "feeling intelligence," and the gut center provides us "doing intelligence."[10] When we employ these intelligence centers, we gain wisdom to discern our lives. We think about our experience, we feel our way through our experience, and we act upon our experience. Here's how:

- Thinking intelligence is used for retrieving and organizing information. It also helps us plan and analyze.
- Feeling intelligence is used for observing emotions in ourselves and others, interpersonal community, and relationship.
- Doing intelligence is used for the movement of our bodies and the body's desires for pleasure and achievement.

Without awareness, we spend much of our time in an over-reliance on one center, supported by another, and misusing or neglecting the third. The flow and rhythm of our ability to know becomes arrhythmic, awkward, and out of sync. In the ancient

Christian tradition, there is a Greek term that captures the essence of the Triune God: *perichoresis*. The term communicates a sense of flow and movement that theologians refer to as the "divine dance" of the three persons of the Trinity, saturated with self-giving love. It's a helpful framework in considering our triadic brain. We need all three to dance together to discern life's decisions effectively.

Our Beautifully Complex and Distributed Mind

Before you write off triadic intelligence as some new age garbage, neuroscience is providing some insight into our ability to know. The human brain is wildly complicated, comprising over 100 billion nerve cells making trillions of connections.[11]

William Schafer, a clinical psychologist, writes that "modern neurology would also tell us that the brain is not located solely in the head but is distributed throughout the body."[12] Scientific researchers, who long considered the brain as more of a central intelligence processing system, are increasingly referring to our brain as a Distributed Intelligence Processing System.[13]

According to scientists Soosalu and Oka, new research identifies neural networks not just in our heads, but also in our hearts and guts. And, they function in highly intelligent ways.[14] To give an example, scientists have identified a network of neurons lining our guts as our "second brain."[15] Such research gives us a lot of insight on what we typically refer to as butterflies in our stomach. According to an article in *Scientific American*:

> Technically known as the enteric nervous system, the second brain consists of sheaths of neurons embedded in the walls of the long tube of our gut, or alimentary canal, which measures about nine meters end to end from the esophagus to the anus. The second brain contains some 100 million neurons . . . [16]

Studies also indicate that our emotions are probably influenced by gut nerves. There's also some intriguing neuroscience work on the heart-brain connection. Neuroscientist Richard Davidson argues that "social and emotional learning can change brain function and actually brain structure and can produce adaptive emotional and cognitive functioning as a consequence."[17]

To be clear, there is much to learn and know about how our cognitive, emotional, and physical systems work together. In the meantime, a basic acknowledgement that our heads, our hearts, and our guts are critical ways of knowing is sufficient to develop a fuller sense of intelligence. Thinking, feeling and doing. Head, heart, and gut. When we learn to trust all three centers of intelligence, we cultivate wisdom.

What does all this have to do with the enneagram? As mentioned earlier a key feature of the enneagram is its perpetual triadic nature. As we consider how our dominant enneagram type impacts our employment of the three centers of intelligence, two specific triadic groupings are helpful: triads and stances. Triads are enneagram types that share a common dominant center of intelligence. Stances are enneagram types that share a common repressed center of intelligence.

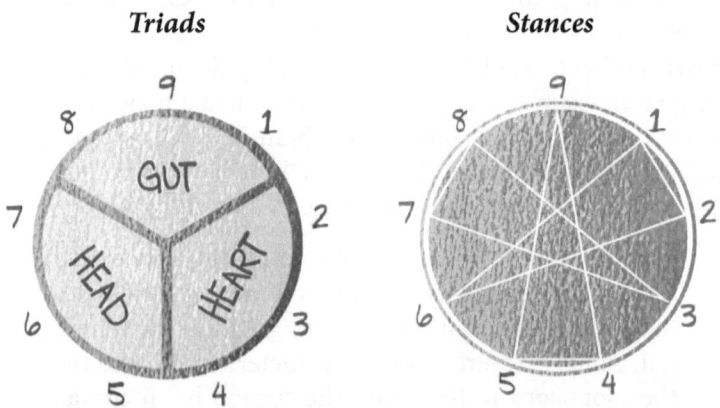

Triads   *Stances*

Let's start with the triads. I'll briefly introduce them, and then we'll explore each type in deeper ways in Part II of the book.

Enneagram Triads: Gut, Heart, and Head

Cognitive Behavioral Therapy is a prominent stream of counseling psychology. It is a psychotherapeutic tool that helps patients better understand the connectedness of thoughts, feelings, and actions. It's informally known as "talk therapy," where a counselor helps a client verbally process through negative, harmful, or disordered thoughts, feelings, and actions.

Thoughts. Feelings. Actions.

Thinking. Feeling. Doing.

This triangle forms a basis of how we live in our world. Together they comprise the building blocks that help (or hinder) our ability to make wise decisions and achieve the results we want in life.

The enneagram similarly provides insight on our thinking, feeling, and doing. Many enneagram teachers begin workshops or trainings by teaching through the "triads," which group enneagram types by their common dominant center of intelligence. Every human being has access to all three centers. However, each enneagram type tends to prefer a center, support it with another center, and neglect or misuse a third center.

As we learned in Chapter One, types Eight, Nine, and One form the Gut Triad and lead with "doing" intelligence. Types Two, Three, and Four form the Heart Triad and lead with "feeling" intelligence.[18] Types Five, Six, and Seven form the Head Triad and lead with "thinking" intelligence. Each type resides in its preferred or leading center of intelligence, and has to more intentionally consider how it uses the other two.

By understanding a dominant personality type's triad and dominant center of intelligence, one gains significant insight into how one perceives their world. When we become more aware of our preferred ways of knowing, we can be more mindful of accessing all three centers more wisely. Neuroscience is now providing evidence of this through the phenomenon of neuroplasticity, the ability to change our brain. My friend Dr. Jerome Lubbe is a functional neurologist and has developed what he calls "The Brain-Based Enneagram." He writes: "Through neuroplasticity…you can reshape and remake how your brain not only functions, but how it continues to develop in the future."[19]

Another helpful way to consider the three centers is the Head Brain, the Heart Brain, and the Gut Brain.[20] To better understand, let's take a closer look at each center.

The Gut Center [Doing]

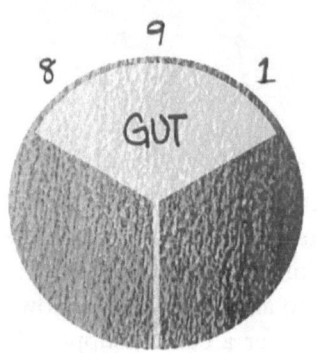

Types Eight, Nine, and One form the Gut Triad. These types tend to be more doing oriented, and let their gut lead in decision-making. Gut Types have loads of intuition and instinctual knowledge. They tend to be more aware of what's going on in their bodies physically, and they sometimes know before they *know*. We all have experiences where we knew something to be true before we had the facts and necessary information before us. As Schafer explains, "When you know something in the body, it seems beyond all doubt."[21] This type of experience is more common among the Gut Types, and is referred to by some as "GQ" or "gut intelligence."[22]

To a certain degree, we all learn by doing. Activity creates momentum. By engaging our bodies in activity, we open up our intelligence viscerally, utilizing sensations and instincts. Of the three centers of intelligence, the Gut Center is the one what helps us be present to what matters. Our minds and hearts can wander, but our bodies are where they are. When we say we can't be in two places at once, it's physically true. When it comes to decision-making, one of the most important strategies is to be present and focused on what matters most. The Gut Center helps us do this.

While the Gut Center helps us be present, this also comes with some challenges. Instinct and intuition can be powerful, but it's not foolproof. Gut Types can be prone to an overreliance on their instincts, forsaking thinking and feeling. They can also mistake gut-level intuition with feeling intelligence. This can truncate the emotional center to mere anger or frustration. In fact, many enneagram teachers attach a common response to anxiety (our common experience of stress) for each triad. For the Gut Triad, anger is that emotion. Each type experiences and responds to anger differently, but Eights, Nines, and Ones all are prone to anger when things go awry.

Gut Types, when not using their thinking and feeling intelligences effectively, can also fall into cycles of over-activity, re-activity, or over-planning. When this occurs, Gut Types often have high demands for themselves and others, and can become more hostile. Type Eights tend to excessively act at the expense of themselves and others. Type Nines tend to forget themselves and retreat to their inner landscape to plan and muse. Type Ones tend to be more reactive, often with a critical bent. Gut Types can be fixated on power and influence, and lose sight of their ability to rest in who they are.

However, when healthy, The Gut Center types are beautiful examples of how to be present, how to trust their own intuition, and how to take the next right step even if they don't have all the information others feel is necessary. This "Gut Brain" is where we find courage to move and act.

The Heart Center [Feeling]

Types Two, Three, and Four form the Heart Triad. These types tend to be more feeling oriented, and are more connected to the emotional world. This allows Twos, Threes, and Fours to access empathy and compassion more easily than other types. The Heart

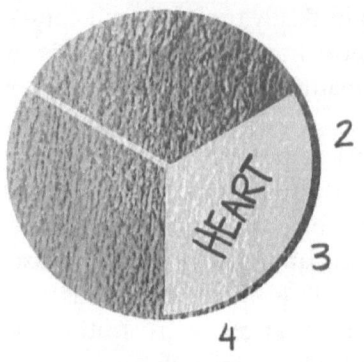

Types are highly relational and care deeply about connectedness. According to Hurley and Donson, for Heart Types, "the most important goal in life is understanding other people."[23] This ability to read people and connect with them conveys an emotional awareness or "EQ," and is described by Calhoun, et al. as "energized by the outer world of relationships."[24]

We can all let our feelings lead the way. Connecting with others in meaningful ways provides an important check to our instinctive reactivity. Instincts are powerful forces, and can sometimes lead to unintended harm to others. Such EQ also helps us more effectively apply our rational/objective thought by considering relational dynamics. We've all crafted ideas that seemed brilliant in our heads, only to fall flat when shared with others. By engaging our heart through listening to and exploring our emotional landscape, we rightly consider the impact we have on others, and the impact others have on us.

While the Heart Center helps us experience emotion, this also comes with some challenges. Feelings are not always the best barometer. Feelings can betray what is truly going on, and when the heart center feels threatened, shame can emerge. Shame is the common response to anxiety for the Heart Triad. Each type experiences and responds to shame differently, but Twos, Threes, and Fours are all prone to it. Type Twos tend to fixate on others' needs and how they can meet them. Type Threes tend to worry about others' perceptions of them as successful or attractive. Type Fours tend to be concerned about their distinctiveness or uniqueness.

Heart Types, when not integrating their doing and thinking intelligences effectively, can also image-craft, manipulate, or become overly sensitive. In a tragic irony, Heart Types can struggle with something they value deeply: authenticity. When their emotional world feels threatened, and shame creeps in, these types will focus too heavily on how others perceive them.

However, when healthy, The Heart Center types are lovely examples of how to connect with others, display empathy, and consider others in important decisions. This "Heart Brain" is where we relate to others and cultivate values to guide our decisions.

The Head Center [Thinking]

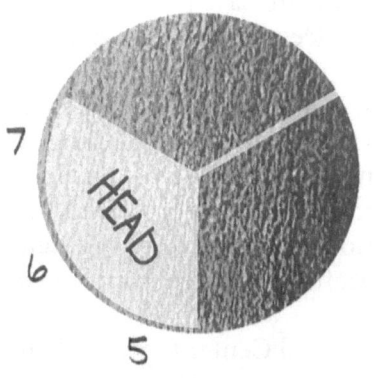

Types Five, Six, and Seven form the Head Triad. These types tend to be more thinking oriented, and tend to let their thoughts dominate decision-making. They are great at harnessing mental faculties to analyze and perceive information. Content is king for Head Types, and generally they don't let emotions or instincts get in the way of their objectivity. If Gut Types major in "GQ" and Heart Types in "EQ," Head Types major in "IQ." According to Calhoun, et al., "The safety and security of our world often ride on the shoulders of head people who know how to gather, analyze, and compute information into plans, strategies, and action."[25] In other words, when there's an important decision to make, Head Types can think their way through it.

The ability to think our way through problems is a critical skill for us all. By engaging our cognitive abilities, we test our feelings against reality. We also slow down our instinctual responses to consider our impulses and evaluate our activity. By employing our head, we learn, critique, consider, and develop important strategies.

Head Types must be careful not to solely rely on their IQ to make their way in the world. While we can think our way through much, we don't always have sufficient information for every situation. Demoting emotions can cause pain and frustration and neglect the wisdom of others. Overanalyzing instincts can delay important action. Head Types can then become anxious about their inability to think their way through. When this occurs, anxiety creeps in and Head Types become prone to fear. Fear takes on different forms for each Head Type. Type Fives tend to retreat and withdraw from others. Type Sixes tend to operate based on worst-case scenarios. Type Sevens tend to flee when things become boring or difficult.

Such fear-based reactions can cause Head Types to double-down on their thinking. Such overthinking is often poor thinking. According to Hurley and Donson, a persistent aspect of Head Types is "their deep-seated unwillingness to accept information from the other two centers."[26] Head Types must be careful to not feel superior to others who lead with GQ or EQ.

However, when healthy, The Head Center types are brilliant examples of how to employ our cognitive abilities to gather information and use it to make wise decisions. This "Head Brain" provides cognition, meaning, and creativity to aid discernment.

Our thoughts, feelings, and actions are powerful tools of discernment. When we lack self-awareness, we rely too heavily upon our dominant center of intelligence and tend to distort or misuse the other two centers. Without some serious work, we simply operate on a mechanical level. In other words, our intelligence is functional and not formational. When we consider vocation, our overuse and underuse of our three centers "distorts our ability to perceive or understand ourselves, others, and life in general."[27]

Our lives are too important to live on autopilot. The goal is to faithfully employ our thinking, doing, and feeling to cultivate wisdom in life. To depend too heavily on your preferred center of intelligence will distort our discernment. To underuse your full range of intelligence will also distort our discernment. This is where a different grouping of enneagram types can be helpful: the Stances.

Enneagram Stances: Aggressive, Dependent, Withdrawn

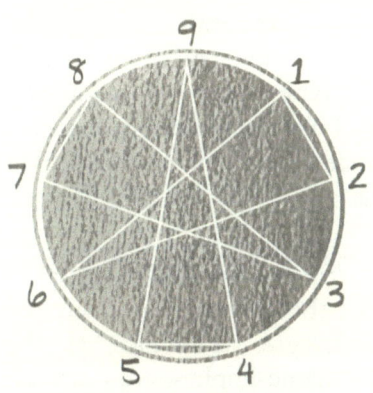

The Stances of the enneagram, sometimes referred to as "social styles" or "Hornevian groups" (a credit to psychologist Karen Horney),[28] provide further insight into how each enneagram type uses the three centers of intelligence. Remember, The Triads help us understand what center each type leads with: Doing Intelligence for Gut Types (Eight, Nine, One), Feeling Intelligence for Heart Types (Two, Three, Four), and Thinking Intelligence for Head Types (Five, Six, Seven).

The Stances of the enneagram are grouped by the center of intelligence that is misused or distorted. Some teachers refer to this as the repressed center of intelligence. I find it helpful to consider the three centers of intelligence playing a game of keep away, with two centers leaving out the third, who rarely gets the ball.

Consistent with the inherent logic of the enneagram's design, the three Stances form identical isosceles triangles, grouping two neighbor types with a third across the circle. Think of it as one edge of an intelligence center pairing with another edge to shoot across the frame to form the triangle.

The three Stances of the enneagram are the Aggressive Stance (types Three, Seven, Eight), the Dependent Stance

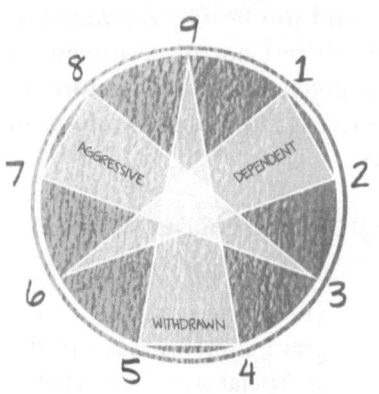

(types One, Two, Six), and the Withdrawn Stance (types Four, Five, Nine). Each Stance draws from two Centers of Intelligence to form a particular way of engaging their world, while neglecting or distorting a third center.

The Stances help us better understand how each type engages its world and tries to solve problems. By identifying each stance's distorted center of intelligence, we can notice the blind spots that inhibit our ability to make wise decisions.

The Aggressive Stance (Types Three, Seven, Eight)

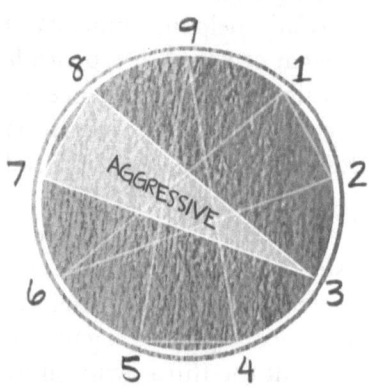

Those who lead from the Aggressive Stance, as the name implies, are more assertive toward others. They tend to "move against" others to get what they want (even if it's not apparent externally, it's often an internal move). Types Three, Seven, and Eight have abundant energy to gain what they desire. They are less affected by the attacks of inner critics, and portray a more defined sense of who they are in the world.

Aggressive Stance types *think* and *do* their way through life, and often neglect or misuse *feeling*. Types Three, Seven, and Eight are strategic, get-things-done people. They tend to look ahead (more on this in Chapter Three) and focus on what's next. This foresight and planning can be very helpful when discerning a path. They can make progress, forge ahead, and build momentum. But often looking ahead can come at the expense of our EQ (emotional intelligence).

When we quiet down our frenetic activity and let our hearts catch up to our bodies we can more fully assess the present. We can also better reflect upon the past. This raises up our EQ in ways that help us better read people and ourselves. When we do, we develop compassion and empathy to use the full range of our intelligence.

But this requires intentional work. Without such work, each type in the Aggressive stance represses or misuses feelings in unique ways. NOTE: This doesn't mean that Threes, Sevens, and Eights don't have feelings. Of course they have feelings. But these Aggressive types have tendencies to neglect or misuse them.

Type Three: Feeling Distorted

Type Threes are great at getting things done and looking good doing it. But Threes struggle to slow down the activity enough to truly engage their own feelings and the feelings of others. This can lead Threes to use people to achieve their goals. It can also prevent them from learning from past mistakes or failures. Such a dismissal of one's own feelings and the feelings of others can lead to a frenetic cycle of seeking value and worth from others rather than authentic connection. Type Threes can overvalue their own accomplishments as a means to compensate for undervaluing healthy relationships. In summary, the value and worth that Threes seek can be found within oneself and within vibrant relationships with others.

Type Seven: Feeling Distorted

Type Sevens thrive at moving from activity to activity. They tend to devote much of their thinking to planning what's next to keep up the adventure or intrigue. This is why Sevens are always up for just about anything. Such activity seems wonderfully (or terrifyingly) spontaneous to non Sevens. In reality, Sevens are quick thinkers and planners. To them, such a move to what's next isn't nearly as spontaneous.

Like Threes, Sevens often move about in the world too fast for their heart to catch up. They can jump quickly to the next thing, especially when the present environment feels boring, painful, sad, or awkward. With one eye perpetually on what's next, they tend to overlook their own feelings and others'. The satisfaction they seek in their activity is fleeting, which causes them to plan for the next, over and over again. If Sevens stick around long enough to acknowledge and engage their feelings and the feelings of others, they'll eventually realize that growth and contentment come from working through pain, not running from it.

Type Eight: Feeling Distorted

Type Eights often seem the most aggressive of the three Aggressive Types. Type Eights can be intensely focused on the task ahead and can bulldoze their way through it. When unchecked, others can feel hurt and discarded in the process. Unhealthy Eights may not care that others get hurt. Many Eights care, but simply don't notice.

This hard-charging nature of Eights tend to pursue activity at the expense of feelings. When feelings do occur in Eights, they can be dark or vengeful, which fuels their ability to operate in terms of conquest. Such a conquering posture maintains a false sense of protection and control. When Eights slow down enough to let their hearts catch up to their heads and bodies, they realize that projecting strength and control doesn't truly protect or control what matters most. By listening to the wisdom of their hearts and the feelings of others, Eights relinquish unnecessary control and feel more protected where they are.

Riso and Hudson tell us that Aggressive types must open their hearts.[29] Aggressive types fall victim to the myth that feelings aren't helpful in discerning the most important questions. They seem wasteful, unproductive, and inefficient. In reality, healthy engagement of our hearts draw us into deeper parts of ourselves, and nudge us toward others in community. When faced with life's most important questions, authentic emotional connections with ourselves and others are essential.

Discernment: What am I feeling?

For those who lead from the Aggressive Stance, restless hearts must become authentic places of emotion and connection. In a word, they must *OPEN* their hearts with vulnerability. Types Three, Seven, and Eight can intentionally form **Wise Hearts** to discern well. This requires intentional work exploring their emotional world, honoring it as a teacher (not just a drag).

The Dependent Stance (Types One, Two, Six)

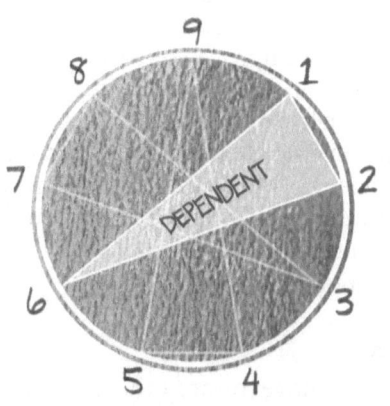

Those who lead from the Dependent Stance, are other-focused. They tend to "move toward" or come alongside others for affection, approval, or belonging. In this way, their sense of self is more flexible, looking to others for definition. These types are compliant to their inner critics, which tends to leave them conflicted internally. Types One, Two, and Six form this stance, and tend to be more dutiful in their engagement with others.

Dependent Stance types *do* and *feel* their way through life, and often neglect or misuse *thinking*. Types One, Two, and Six are often dependent upon others to get things done. They tend to look at what's right in front of them (more on this in Chapter Three) and focus on the here and now. This often thwarts productive foresight and planning that is essential when discerning a path. They can suffer from the tyranny of the urgent and often neglect their own IQ (thinking intelligence).

When we take a deep breath and assess what we truly want and need, we can more fully plan for the future. This accesses our IQ in ways that help us better plan and prepare. When we do, we develop a calm confidence and healthy ambition by using the full range of our intelligence.

Like most (if not all) worthwhile things, this takes work. Without some honest work, Dependent Types can neglect or misuse their thinking intelligence in some unique ways. NOTE: This doesn't mean that Ones, Twos, and Sixes are less intelligent than the other numbers. Rather, they have pronounced tendencies to misuse the IQ they possess. Here's how.

Type One: Thinking Distorted

Type Ones are in the continuous quality improvement business. They perpetually scan for ways to make things better. They are partial to practical ideas and solutions that just seem to make sense. They feel deeply about how to improve something, and set about the task of doing it. This can lead to a busyness that thwarts open-minded inquiry and self-care.

Ones tend to improve what's around them as a way to cope with their own feelings of deficiency. Thus, their thinking is often dominated by their own inner critic. By quieting the mind to think more productively and authentically, Ones can see that the goodness they care so much about is within.

Type Two: Thinking Distorted

If Ones tend to improve, Type Twos move toward others to help. They instinctively feel when someone has need, and set about helping. Riso and Hudson describe Twos as those who "do their feelings."[30] Those who lead with Type Two act almost instinctively upon their feelings, often without much thinking.

When Twos take the time to pause and think about what they feel before they act, they provide a clearer boundary between feeling and doing. Such thinking also helps Twos evaluate where and when to help others. When they do, they can more clearly experience love for who they are, not what they do. They can then employ their helping skills with wisdom.

Type Six: Thinking Distorted

Type Sixes are prone to move toward others to feel secure. This leads Sixes to depend on others for guidance and support. When the present environment feels at all threatening, Sixes are prone to focus on mitigating the threat. This "batten down the hatches" mentality prepares for scenarios that often are unlikely, and uses energy better served for more hopeful planning.

To get out of feeling insecure, doing-things-to-feel-more-secure cycle, Sixes must learn to trust their own thinking and intuition. They must decrease their tendency to think through threat-forecasting and instead trust themselves to be free to plan, dream, and strategize about good things.

Again, those who lead with One, Two, or Six are not dumb; not in the least. However, they tend to limit their thinking in ways that curb their ability to discern well. By opening their minds, Dependent Types find agency to lift their gaze out of the present deficiencies, needs, or insecurities to consider life with more vantage.

Discernment: What am I thinking?

Those who lead from the Dependent Stance must find ways to focus their racing minds into poised, salient thinking. In word, they must *TRUST* their heads. Types One, Two, and Six can cultivate **Wise Heads** to think creatively and strategically about important decisions. Deepen thinking beyond the tyranny of the urgent to discern what is truly needed.

The Withdrawn Stance (Types Four, Five, Nine)

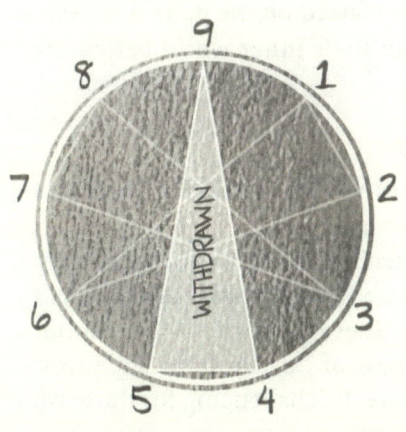

We all can point to times when we needed others to help us find our way. The important people in our lives inspire us to move and act. The Withdrawn Stance types are more distant from others, and often, distant from their authentic selves. They tend to move away from others, valuing privacy, space, and independence. This wariness can often be sold as solitude, but it's important to know that withdrawing is not the same as solitude. Karen Horney puts it this way: "They (withdrawn types) draw around themselves a kind of magic circle which no one may penetrate."[31] Their sense of self become defined by the barrier more than what it protects. A tendency to isolate can further thwart discernment and estrange those who lead with Four, Five, or Nine from others. Withdrawing on its own is a reactive act, and wisdom is rarely present in reactivity. Solitude has aspects of withdrawal, but is proactive. Wisdom is often cultivated in intention.

If the Aggressive Stance moves in the world with a ready, fire, aim approach to life, the Withdrawing Stance can operate from a ready, aim. . . approach. Sometimes in life, we simply have to discern as we go, something challenging for Withdrawn Types. These types often think and feel their way through life, at the expense of right action. This doesn't mean that they do nothing (although sometimes this is the case). Often, Withdrawn Types do everything BUT the very thing they should do. These types tend to long for what was and what could be, often at the expense of what is (Again, more on this in Chapter Three). They are astute in their reflection and their vision, but struggle to get started on the path. They often feel they need to work through their inner world before they can act. Here's how:

Type Four: Doing Distorted

Those who lead with Type Four have close and ready access to the full range of emotion. When confronted with seemingly overwhelming emotion, they tend to withdraw to think about their feelings, and avoid doing.[32] This thinking often leads to what is missing, or incomplete. These thinking-fueled emotions can bait the Type Four into traps of inferiority or superiority. With all this going on, it can be really challenging for those who lead with Type Four to move to action.

However, this ability to think and feel with such depth and richness provides the Type Four with deep wells of empathy, aesthetic sensibilities, and meaning. When they employ these gifts to what's right in front of them, present to what matters most, the spell breaks and they can fully engage the present moment with wisdom.

Type Five: Doing Distorted

Type Five is the most "heady" in the Withdrawn Stance. When Type Four engages in thinking-fueled emotion, Type Five employs emotion-fueled thinking.[33] Those who lead with Type Five are often described as always "in their heads." Their need for competency will compel them to retreat to a place where their minds can work, and they often won't emerge until they feel competent enough for what's next.

This causes those who lead with Type Five to struggle to initiate; there's always more to know first. It's important for the Type Five to embrace the learning and competency that comes from doing. Experience is a powerful teacher, often more so than study. Wisdom comes from being embodied and grounded in our worlds, rather than escaping from it to the palace of our minds.

Type Nine: Doing Distorted

Those who lead with Type Nine want peace, and they are so committed to it they will withdraw from disruption to maintain it. The Type Nine has an uncanny ability to be physically present in a room, but internally withdrawn to another place. Such a reaction isn't authentic peace. Rather, it's a version of calm that gets us through the momentary conflict.

For those who lead with Type Nine, this extends to even withdrawing from the possibility of disruption or conflict. Which, understandably, keeps a Type Nine right where they are: stuck at the starting line of the race they should be running. This doesn't mean Nines are sedentary. Often they are incredibly busy doing things that aren't all that important, but help them avoid the disruptive activity that awaits them. There's a deeper, lasting peace that is forged in the fire of well engaged conflict. By engaging in right doing, Nines can find it.

The Withdrawn Types are highly skilled at moving away from others and thus, not acting on what matters most. Sometimes the withdrawal is physical. Those who lead with Type Four, Five, or Nine can disappear from a party or meeting like a ghost. Sometimes the withdrawal is internal, physically going through the motions. By engaging the body in doing what needs to be done, Fours, Fives, and Nines access an active wisdom that helps them make sense of their thoughts and emotions.

Discernment: What am I doing?

Those who lead from the Withdrawn Stance must find ways to align their heads and their hearts in their bodies. In a word, they must *EMBODY* their environments. Types Four, Five, and Nine can cultivate **Wise Bodies** to listen to their instincts and act when necessary.

A Quick Aside: The Anchor Points

You may notice that my description of the Triads (types that share the same dominant intelligence) and Stances (types that share the same distorted intelligence) has some seeming contradictions. For those who lead with Types Three, Six, and Nine, the Triads and Stances tell us that these types lead with the very intelligence they distort. How can this be?

Some teachers refer to this triangle of types as the Anchor Points of the Enneagram. Each of these types is in the middle of its Triad. Type Three is in the middle of the Heart Triad, Type Six is in the middle of the Head Triad, and Type Nine is the middle of the Gut Triad. And yet, each distorts that same intelligence. There are a few theories as to why this is. Rather than taking the time needed to explore them all, consider how each distorts its own dominant intelligence:[34]

- *Type Three leads with feeling, but quickly converts it to intel to impress, achieve, and succeed (reading a room to determine who is most important or influential, rather than developing empathy).*

- *Type Six leads with thinking but quickly converts it to threat-forecasting, worst-case scenarios, and plans to secure (making safety plans rather than trusting their intuition that everything will be okay).*
- *Type Nine leads with doing but quickly converts it to doing all sorts of things but that which needs to be done (cleaning the bathroom instead of finishing that report for work, for example).*[35]

In other words, each of these types leads with a form of intelligence, but reject its appropriate use. In tragic irony, Threes become even more detached from their hearts, Sixes become even more detached from their minds, and Nines become even more detached from their bodies. The result is something they all share in common: a sort of conformist-people-pleasing to what each type feels is safest: to be impressive for Threes, to be safe for Sixes, and to be calm for Nines. For those who lead with these types, wise use of the very intelligences they distort is challenging, but essential work.

Conclusion:

The Wisdom Triad spans the full range of intelligence available to each of us:

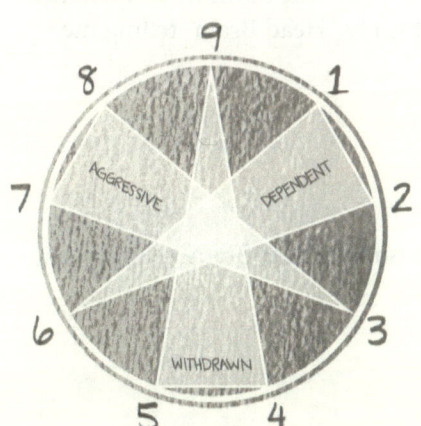

- What am I doing?
- What am I feeling?
- What am I thinking?

Discernment demands this full range: thinking, feeling, and doing. The good news is that we are smarter than we think we are. With intention and work we can employ our bodies, our hearts, and our minds to decisions big and small. The enneagram helps us see the ways in which our personality limits our ability to cultivate wisdom and apply it.

Riso and Hudson teach us that each center provides qualities of our essential and authentic nature that personality is simply trying to imitate.[36] For the Aggressive Stance, those who lead with Three, Seven, or Eight must find ways to open their restless hearts toward authenticity to develop *Wise Hearts*. For the Dependent Stance, those who lead with One, Two, or Six must find ways to trust their racing minds to develop *Wise Heads*. For the Withdrawn Stance, those who lead with Four, Five, or Nine must embody their world to develop *Wise Bodies*.

Many enneagram teachers who work with the intelligence centers talk about the need for balance. I find this problematic as it can create an unhealthy expectation to use all three centers all the time, full throttle. A healthier, more realistic approach to align the intelligence centers is to develop healthy rhythms of doing, feeling, and thinking. In this triadic dance, rhythmic alignment of all three centers cultivates the wisdom to discern.

Exercises:

Your Triadic Brain

- For three days in a row, track ways in which each intelligence center helps you know. Write down what you notice.
    - Day 1—What is my "Head Brain" telling me about my day?

    - Day 2—What is my "Heart Brain" telling me about my day?

o   Day 3—What is my "Gut Brain" telling me about my day?

- For day four, try to notice when your triadic brain is working together. For example, an upset stomach connected to anxious thoughts about an upcoming meeting at work. What do you notice?

Aggressive Stance (Threes, Sevens, Eights):
- An important word for those who lead from the Aggressive Stance is OPEN, specifically calling for an opening of the heart. Spend time throughout a day (or even better, a week), considering your feelings that emerge during your daily activities. Sit with those feelings for a bit (longer than you usually do). Find someone close to you (close friend, spouse, family member) and practice opening your heart by sharing what you notice.
- **Wise Hearts**—Find a few people you trust who aren't in the Aggressive Stance. Ask them the following questions: *How do your feelings help you make wise decisions?* Write down what you learn and try it.

Dependent Stance (Ones, Twos, Sixes)
- An important word for those who lead from the Dependent Stance is TRUST, specifically calling for a trust in sound thinking. Interrogate your inner critic (or, perhaps, committee). Ask questions, such as, is this critic trustworthy? If I don't trust in this inner voice, what would be more trustworthy? Also, consider your trust level of those around you compared to the level of trust you place in yourself. Are you giving yourself enough credit? Are you giving others enough credit?

- **Wise Minds**—Consider recent events in which you fully showed up and everything turned out okay. Consider recent events in which you didn't need others to be ok, finish the job, or find security. What can you learn from this?

Withdrawn Stance (Fours, Fives, Nines)

- An important word for those who lead from the Withdrawn Stance is EMBODY, specifically calling for full presence and participation in their world. Consider ways (even simple ones) in which you can use your body in a given situation. Before retreating from something difficult, painful, or awful, take stock of what your body is telling you before you get into a head and heart space.
- **Wise Bodies**—What physical activity can you engage (exercise, breathing, stretching, power poses) in that would help you develop a Wise Body?

Notes

[1] Serge Benhayon, *An Open Letter to Humanity: A Treatise on Energetic Truth* (Goonellabah, New South Wales, Australia: UniMed Publishing, 2013), p. 287.

[2] T.S. Eliot, *The Rock* (Boston: Harcourt Brace and Company, 1934), p. 7.

[3] Arthur Zajonc, interviewed by Krista Tippett in March 12, 2015, *On Being with Krista Tippett.* https://onbeing.org/programs/arthur-zajonc-michael-mccullough-mind-and-morality-a-dialogue/.

[4] Greek language help here from the NET Bible https://netbible.org.

[5] David Benner, *Surrender to Love: Discovering the Heart of Christian Spirituality* (Downers Grove: InterVarsity Press, 2015), p. 92.

[6] Benner, *Surrender to Love*, p. 93.

[7] James K.A. Smith, *You are What You Love: The Spiritual Power of Habit* (Grand Rapids: Brazos Press, 2016).

[8] Kathy Hurley and Theodorre Donson, *Discover Your Soul Potential: Using the Enneagram to Awaken Spiritual Vitality* (Lakewood, CO: WindWalker Press, 2012), p. 15.

[9] Suzanne Stabile introduced me to this concept in one of her workshops, for which I'm eternally grateful. I've heard other enneagram teachers use it since.

[10] Hurley and Donson, *Discover your Soul Potential*, p. 20.

[11] Kyra Ward, "Neuroscience the Enneagram Part 1: The Link Between Neuroscience and Coaching" (June 21, 2019), https://www.integrative9.com/.

[12] William M. Schafer, *Roaming Free Inside the Cage: A Daoist Approach to the Enneagram* (Bloomington: iUniverse, 2010), p. 6.

[13] For an example of a study of the brain as a Distributed Intelligent Processing System, check out https://www.ncbi.nlm.nih.gov/pmc/articles/PMC3057967/.

[14] G. Soosalu and M. Oka, (2012), "Neuroscience and the Three Brains of Leadership," http://www.mbraining.com/mbit-and-leadership).

[15] https://www.scientificamerican.com/article/gut-second-brain/.

[16] Ibid.

[17] https://www.edutopia.org/video/heart-brain-connection-neuroscience-social-emotional-and-academic-learning.

[18] By "feeling intelligence," I don't mean to include all feelings we experience. For example, the feeling of being cold, or constipated, is not directly tied to emotions. I consider feeling intelligence similarly to emotional intelligence. Feeling intelligence is used more broadly among enneagram teachers, so I use the term to maintain integrity within enneagram teaching.

[19] Jermoe Lubbe, *Whole-Identity: A Brain Baised Enneagram Model for (W)holistic Human Thriving* (Atlanta: Thrive Neuro Theology, 2019), p. 4.

[20] Anna-Rosa Le Roux, "Neuroscience and the Enneagram Part 3: Neuroscientific Evidence for the Enneagram Three Centers of Intelligence," July 25, 2019, https://www.integrative9.com/.

[21] William M. Schafer, *Roaming Free Inside the Cage: A Daoist Approach to the Enneagram*, p. 8.

[22] Adele & Doug Calhoun, Clare and Scott Lougrige, *Spiritual Rhythms of the Enneagram: A Handbook for Harmony and Transformation* (Downer's Grove: IVP, 2019), p. 18.

[23] Kathleen V. Hurley & Theodorre E. Dobson, *What's My Type?: Use the Enneagram System of Nine Personality Types to Discover Your Best Self* (San Francisco: Harper SanFrancisco, 1991), p. 73.

[24] Calhoun, Calhoun, Loughrige, & Loughrige, *Spiritual Rhythms of the Enneagram: A Handbook for Harmony and Transformation*, p. 74.

[25] Ibid, p. 130.

[26] Hurley & Dobson, p. 75.

[27] Ibid, p. 71.

[28] The Enneagram Stances or social styles are sometimes called Hornevian Groups because they derive from the work of psychologist Karen Horney, who theorized that children cultivated three distinct coping strategies: expansive, submission/self-effacement, resignation/detachment. Based off of her work, Enneagram teachers employed and mod-

ified Horney's typology to further understand how enneagram types engage others (aggressive, dependent, and withdrawn).

[29] Riso and Hudson, *Understanding the Enneagram: the Practical Guide to Personality Types Revised Edition* (New York: Houghton Mifflin, 2000), p. 277.

[30] Ibid, p. 258.

[31] Karen Horney, *Our Inner Conflicts: A Constructive Theory of Neurosis* (New York: W. W. Norton, 1945), p. 75.

[32] Risso and Hudson, in *Understanding the Enneagram*, have some really helpful content about the interplay of thinking and feeling in Type Four.

[33] Again, Riso and Hudson, *Understanding the Enneagram*.

[34] Thanks to the teachings of Suzanne Stabile and the written works of Kathy Hurley and Theodorre Donson for helping make sense of this. Note: Theodorre Donson has written under the surname "Dobson" and "Donson."

[35] Suzanne Stabile often uses similar language about the Type Nine throughout her writings and teachings.

[36] Riso and Hudson, *Understanding the Enneagram*, p. 250.

CHAPTER FOUR

The Practice Triad: Past, Present, Future

"All we have to decide is what to do with the time that is given us."
—J.R.R. Tolkien, *The Fellowship of the Ring*

It seems to hit me about once a month. Despite my best efforts to manage my calendar and leave some breathing room to avoid turning into some soulless worker-robot, I'll have a day where my schedule is packed from the beginning of the workday till the end. Inevitably, my first appointment of the day will run ten minutes late, forcing me to play a cruel and sadistic game of catch-up every hour on the hour. I enter each room breathless and apologetic, and end the day in a daze of frustration. The commute home causes me to wish "if only I had more time."

Western approaches to time reside in a place of scarcity. We're always running out of time. And yet, time is elastic: the days feel full but the years, in retrospect, are short. We often feel that we have too much to do in any given day, but we look back over the course of a year and wonder, "Where did all the time go?"

We live in a cultural moment in the West in which we have an abundance of technology to help us be more efficient and productive. Productivity seminars, techniques, apps, and the like all contribute to what Melissa Gregg referred to as "The Productivity Obsession."[1] Google "productivity" and you'll find about 18 million results. (Reading through them all doesn't seem that productive).

A century ago, Max Weber observed that the Protestant ethic believed that the "waste of time is the first and in principle the deadliest of sins."[2] Yet, this pension for productivity hacks and efficiency techniques seem to have the opposite effect.

We even subconsciously reveal the madness of our busyness obsession in our interactions with others. A simple, "How are you?" often results in: "I'm crazy busy." Our obsession with productivity is affecting us in profound ways.

We now are busier than ever, more stressed, and more connected to work through emails, messaging apps, and social media.

We haven't found a way to create more time. But we continue to find ways to spend it toward less important ends.

When we do this, we enter into a frenetic life guided by what our calendar apps tell us to do. We simply wander from event to event and lose a sense of wholeness. Our lives become a packed list of appointments and meetings on our calendar app. We search for meaning and significance in the escapes.

To take stock of how we spend the time that comprises our days and our weeks is a daunting task. When we do, we are confronted with two truths found in the arts:

Where you invest your love, you invest your life
—Mumford and Sons[3]

How we spend our days is, of course, how we spend our lives
—Annie Dillard[4]

While time machines and science fiction tales of bending the space-time continuum are tempting, we don't really need more time to live a good and faithful life. In fact, we have all the time we need. We have all the time we're going to get. What we need is greater depth in our time. What we need is better stewardship of our time. . .not to be more efficient or productive, but *to be more faithful.*

The Enneagram of Discernment encourages us to live life in the *fullness* of the time available to us. To discern deeply, we must have a full perspective of time. A full perspective includes engaging the following questions:

- *What am I remembering?* This question engages our past.
- *What am I experiencing?* This question engages our present.
- *What am I anticipating?* This question engages our future.

Minutes vs. Moments

This full perspective of time requires us to think less about quantity, and more about quality. The ancient Greeks have something to teach us on this. They had two words for time: *chronos* time and *kairos* time. *Chronos* time refers to ordinary, chronological time: seconds, minutes, hours, days, weeks, months, years, etc.

Kairos time is different. In the ancient Greek, the word refers to a right, critical, or opportune time.

Chronos time is essentially quantitative. It's finite. It's easily defined and measured…by minutes.

Kairos time is, in essence, qualitative. It's infinite. It's more easily experienced than defined. It's immeasurable…captured in moments.

In the New Testament, *kairos* is used 86 times, utilizing this expansive depth of time to refer to the appointed time in the purpose of God. [5]

Chronos is ordinary time.

Kairos is EXTRAordinary time.

We too often operate our lives in *chronos* time (minutes) in ways that thwart *kairos* time (moments).

But discernment and transformation occur in *kairos* moments.

Discerning cannot simply be done in *chronos* time. The moments of clarity, the glimmers of insight, and the rays of vision of our calling come in *kairos* time.

This isn't to say we can escape *chronos* time. Humanity is bound by it. It's irrefutable. But, we can use our ordinary time in more purposeful ways. We can make way for *kairos* moments when we utilize all three perspectives on time: past, present, and future.

When we have a deep understanding of how our past shapes us. . .

When we truly pay attention to our present . . .

When we do what is needed to be prepared for our future. . .

We make ourselves more available to the work of God in *kairos* time.

Etymological studies trace origins of *kairos* to archery; the moment when an arrow may be fired to hit a target. This minute, chronologically, is no different than any other minute in an archer's day. This minute contains that same amount of seconds as any other. But when an archer steadies her bow, pulls back the string to the "anchor point," and calms her breathing, this is the *kairos* moment. There's a weight and gravity in this moment. The attention, the focus, the steadiness, the wind, the force of the bow, the pointing of the arrow all create the condition for hitting the target.

Discernment is a lifelong practice of devoting our *chronos* time to listening to the call of God in the *kairos* moments.

Personality and Perspective on Time

How do we utilize all three perspectives on time to practice discernment? How do we listen to the past, stay present, and be prepared for the future? The Enneagram of Discernment provides insight into how each type utilizes time. Think of our overall perspective on time as another three-person dance, requiring alignment and rhythm; one dance partner is the past, one is the present, and one is the future. Each type has a tendency to put most of its focus on a dominant perspective to time, supported by another perspective on time, while neglecting a third. In other words, when we dance, we are prone to leave a partner out.

But, when we develop rhythms of practice in the fullness of time, seeking the wisdom of the past, the present, and the future, we make ourselves more available and ready for discernment.

In the last chapter, we looked briefly at triads and stances. Key to understanding your perspective on time are the enneagram's Stances (Chapter Three). Each enneagram Stance type has a dominant perspective to time, a supporting perspective to time, and a repressed perspective to time.[6]

Remember, there are three stances within the enneagram:

- The dependent stance (1, 2, 6)
- The aggressive stance (3, 7, 8)
- The withdrawn stance (4, 5, 9)

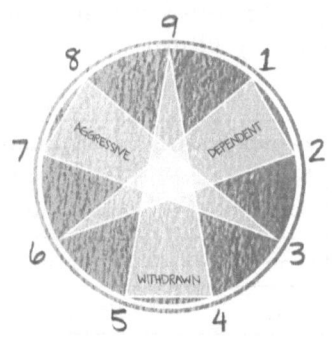

Each stance shares some common characteristics that we explored in the previous chapter. Each of us has all three intelligences (thinking, feeling, doing) available to us, but we're prone to lead with one intelligence center, support it with another, and distort the third.[7]

Stances are groups of types that share in common the ways in which they interpret their world, analyze it, and process it. In other words, stances are the primary postures we take when we engage the world and try to solve its problems. These stances are also marked by their posture in engaging others. This is not about introversion or extroversion. Rather, it's a posture toward others that flows from our internal motivations and can exhibit external behaviors, regardless of how outgoing you are.

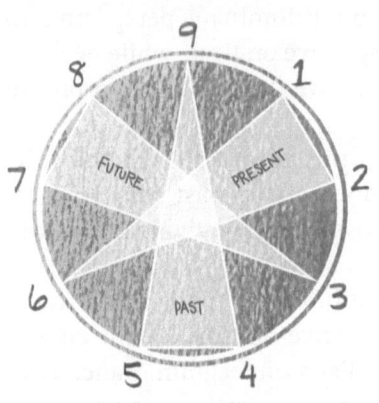

Let's begin with the Stances' dominant perspectives on time:

The types in the Aggressive Stances (Three, Seven, Eight) are future oriented. The types in the Dependent Stance (One, Two, Six) are present oriented. The Types in the Withdrawn Stance (Four, Five, Nine) are past oriented. Similar to the intelligence centers, each type tends to support this orientation with another perspective, while neglecting a third:

Enneagram Number	Dominant Perspective to Time	Supporting Perspective to Time	Neglected Perspective to Time
One	Present	Past	Future
Two	Present	Past	Future
Three	Future	Present	Past
Four	Past	Future	Present
Five	Past	Future	Present
Six	Present	Past	Future
Seven	Future	Present	Past
Eight	Future	Present	Past
Nine	Past	Future	Present

When we combine what we've learned about the intelligence centers with this approach to time perspectives, we begin to see some patterns that affect the ability to discern well.

The Practice Triad: Past, Present, Future

Enneagram Stance	Distorted Center of Intelligence	Posture in engaging others	Neglected perspective to time
Dependent (1, 2, 6)	Thinking	Move toward	Future
Aggressive (3, 7, 8)	Feeling	Move against	Past
Withdrawn (4, 5, 9)	Doing	Move away	Present

The connections between a Stance's distorted center of intelligence and neglected perspective to time may not be apparent right away, but with some further explanation they make perfect sense. Let's explore each Stance to discover how.

Dependent Stance (One, Two, Six)

Enneagram Number	Preferred Perspective to Time	Supporting Perspective to Time	Neglected Perspective to Time
One (Reformer)	Present	Past	Future
Two (Helper)	Present	Past	Future
Six (Loyalist)	Present	Past	Future

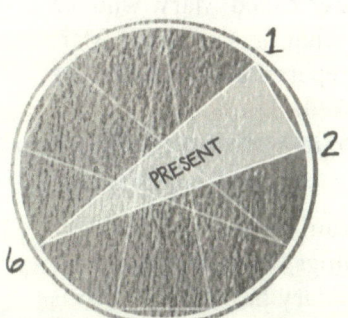

Remember, those in the dependent stance focus more on the external world and other people rather than themselves. This is also known as the "moving toward" stance. Those in the Dependent Stance rely primarily on doing and feeling intelligence and distort thinking intelligence.

In other words, they often struggle to productively think their way through a situation.

This is directly related to their orientation toward time. Ones, Twos and Sixes prefer to be *present* focused. They tend to fixate on what is presently before them either to improve (ones), help (twos), or secure (sixes). To support this present mindset, dependent numbers also rely on the past as their supporting perspective to time. The past informs the reforming motivation of ones, the helping motivation of twos, and the securing motivation of sixes as they move toward others.

What's great about this stance is that you typically don't need to worry whether or not dependent numbers will act in the present moment. They are highly responsive to needs in their midst. Also, they let the past inform their perspective on how to respond. They utilize the past as a teacher, which equips and empowers their present responses to situations.

However, the dependent numbers have a tendency to focus on the present, informed by the past at the expense of the future. When the future is repressed, they can be the ones rearranging the deck chairs on the titanic while it's sinking.

This tension is illustrated in Luke 10:38-42, where Jesus visits the home of Martha and Mary:

At the Home of Martha and Mary

[38]As Jesus and his disciples were on their way, he came to a village where a woman named Martha opened her home to him. [39]She had a sister called Mary, who sat at the Lord's feet listening to what he said. [40]But Martha was distracted by all the preparations that had to be made. She came to him and asked, "Lord, don't you care that my sister has left me to do the work by myself? Tell her to help me!"

[41]"Martha, Martha," the Lord answered, "you are worried and upset about many things, [42]but few things are needed—or indeed only one. Mary has chosen what is better, and it will not be taken away from her."

When not aligned or healthy, dependent numbers struggle to productively think what present needs are truly most important, and how tending to those needs will impact the future. Without a healthy and balanced perspective, dependent stances are prone to be like Martha, distracted by all that needs to be done. A more balanced perspective on time for dependent stances would be Mary: sitting at the feet of Jesus; a much more important preparation for the future.

In this way, dependent numbers are dependent on their response to others. This reactionary approach to life often leaves them trapped in the present.

More specifically, here is how each dependent number may neglect a future perspective to time.

Type Ones

- "I can't plan for next week with my apartment in such disarray. I can't focus on what's next until I fix/solve the problems of right now."

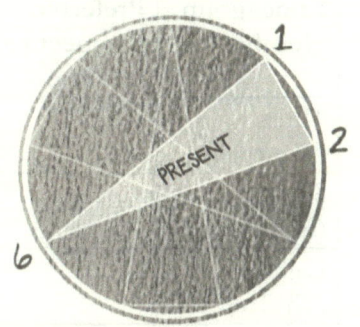

Type Twos

- "There's just too much need around me right now to focus on what I need to get ready for."

Type Sixes

- "I can't focus on the future until I have my bases covered. Once I feel safe, secure and certain about right now I'll think about what's next."

Dependent numbers must realize that time and energy spent on the future is not wasteful or indulgent. Rather, a clearer vision of the future provides some healthy checks and balances to the present. It also provides an important avenue for the wisdom of past experience to be applied.

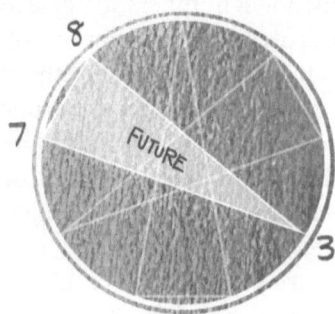

Discernment: What am I anticipating?

To bring their perspectives on time in balance, dependent numbers must cultivate a *Sacred Vision*; a Spirit-led look to the future that draws upon the wisdom of the past and the attention to the present. This requires an honest approach to anticipation.

Aggressive Stance (Three, Seven, Eight)

Enneagram Number	Preferred Perspective to Time	Supporting Perspective to Time	Neglected Perspective to Time
Three (Achiever)	Future	Present	Past
Seven (Enthusiast)	Future	Present	Past
Eight (Challenger)	Future	Present	Past

As we learned in Chapter Two, this stance is also known as the "moving against" stance. These types focus on gaining what they desire. They think clearly about what they want and then *assert oneself* (even if it's internal assertion) through action to get it. Those in the Aggressive Stance rely primarily on thinking and doing intelligence, and distort feeling intelligence. In other words, they often set aside or misuse feelings to get the job done or stay positive.

This repression of feeling intelligence impacts aggressive numbers' perspective to time by pushing feelings aside to focus on what needs to get done or what can be experienced. Reflecting on the past takes time and requires confronting feelings about the past, both good and bad. This gets in the way of efficiency and productivity. This distortion of feelings also impacts the present. To cope, aggressive numbers tend to only stay present enough to accomplish what they want to in order to get to what's next on the list of tasks, problems, or adventures. So, aggressive numbers prefer a future perspective to time in which they always have one eye on what's next. This future perspective is supported by a present perspective to time, devoting enough energy and focus to get the next thing done to move on. What's left behind (pun intended) is the past.

What's great about the aggressive numbers is that you don't have to worry about their lack of planning. They can be efficient, productive, and can conquer a to-do list. They can be decisive and can move quickly.

But this *ready, then fire, and then maybe aim* approach has consequences. An unwillingness to reflect or learn from the past will make aggressive numbers prone to repeat mistakes. This impulsivity can cause aggressive numbers to make rash decisions without properly tending to their own feelings and the feelings of those around them. In addition, aggressive numbers are present, but not fully so. They are present to the task at hand, but always gearing up for what's next. This often means that they struggle to stay focused and present in relationships with others.

This tension of dismissing the past is powerfully illustrated in a number of scientific studies of the brain that indicate that our ability to effectively imagine the future depends on the same neural parts of our brain that remember the past. In other words, our ability to store information from the past is critical to imagine future events.[8]

Aggressive numbers struggle to be honest with their feelings and the feelings of others. This leads them to shut off critical reflection of the past, which thwarts the past's ability to shape how aggressive numbers can live into the future. A more balanced perspective devotes time and energy to mining the riches of the past for wisdom to guide one into the future. This requires aggressive numbers not only to pause and reflect more, but also to be more honest and authentic with their feelings, both good and bad, suffering and joy, failure and success.

Eloise Ristad wrote, "When we give ourselves permission to fail, we, at the same time, give ourselves permission to excel."[9] Permission to fail requires risk, requires grace of ourselves, and requires an acknowledgment that we don't always measure up to our own high standards. Our past failures are teachable moments . . . opportunities for growth that are essential to our future achievement.

More specifically, here's how each aggressive type struggles to bring a past perspective to time into alignment with the present and future:

Type Threes

- "I can't dwell on the past. Don't have time. Look at this list! I need to get this one thing done so I can get to the six other things on the list before tomorrow."

Type Sevens

- "I begged my boss to let me take this project. I had no idea how long it would take. You know what, I need a breather. Wanna go get a cup of coffee with me?"

Type Eights

- "I don't have time to hear my coworker drone on and on about last week's meeting with corporate. Such a waste of time."

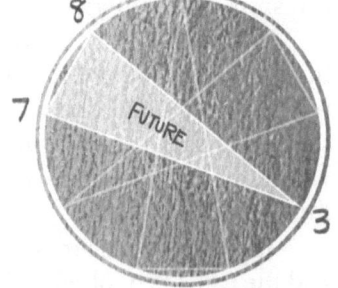

Aggressive numbers must realize that the past is a powerful teacher, with much wisdom to offer both the present challenge at hand, and the future ones ahead.

The Practice Triad: Past, Present, Future

Discernment: What am I remembering?

To bring their perspectives on time in balance, aggressive numbers must cultivate the *Sacred Delay*, a proactive pause to wait and reflect upon the past and sit in the feelings that come with it. This requires an honest approach to remembering.

Withdrawn Stance (Four, Five, Nine)

Enneagram Number	Preferred Perspective to Time	Supporting Perspective to Time	Neglected Perspective to Time
Four	Past	Future	Present
Five	Past	Future	Present
Nine	Past	Future	Present

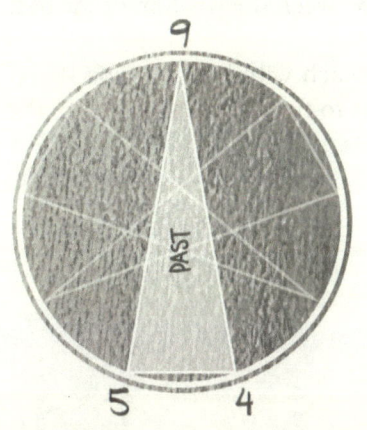

Those in the Withdrawn Stance are characterized by "moving away" from people. These types are highly imaginative, focusing on thinking and feeling. Those in the Withdrawing Stance rely primarily on thinking and feeling intelligence, and repress doing intelligence. In other words, they often struggle to initiate action, especially the most important thing that needs to be done. This doesn't mean they don't do anything. Rather, they are often very busy with anything and everything but the one thing they should be doing.

This distortion of doing intelligence directly relates to their preferred time perspective: the past. Withdrawing numbers can get stuck in the past, posing a significant challenge for the present. In fact, withdrawing numbers will very easily dwell on the past and then leap right over the present to dream about the future. This can cause these types to retreat into themselves in isolating and escapist ways.

What's great about withdrawing numbers is that they are able to see the complexity in any situation. Desire for uniqueness (fours), objectivity (fives), and peace (nines) compel them to take time to reflect, ponder, feel, and explore complexities. They are able to see things from many angles.

However, they can get caught in the vicious cycle of musing on what was and daydreaming about what could be. In so doing, they neglect what IS. When they neglect what IS, they neglect what can be done in the here and now.

It's important for withdrawn types to let the past shape, but not define. It's also important to know that engagement in the present is the best preparation for the future. To be fully present to the things that truly matter will prepare and equip you for the future. The present is the bridge between the wisdom of the past and the potential of the future.

More specifically, here's how each withdrawing type struggles to bring a present perspective to time into balance with the past and the future.

Type Fours

- "I don't think I'm up for going out. I need some more time to work through a few things. I don't really know some of the people anyway, so I'm not sure we'd click. Can we postpone?"

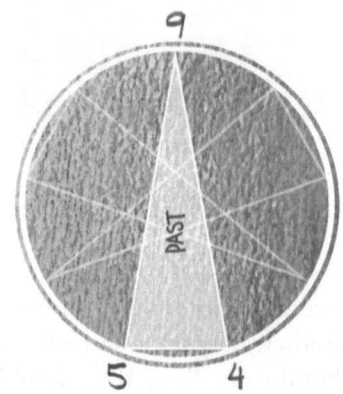

Type Fives

- "I don't have the time or energy to meet with you. I need to make some progress on this idea I've been working on. Lots of reading and researching to do. I need to find a quiet place to hole up and think."

Type Nines

- "Stressful meeting on the calendar today at work and I'm not feeling 100%. I really should be on top of my game, so it's probably better to take a day to regroup."

Withdrawing numbers must realize that the past and future are simply the abstract without the present; and the present provides essential context and meaning to our thoughts and feelings.

Discernment: What am I experiencing?

To bring their perspectives on time in balance, withdrawing numbers must cultivate a *Sacred Presence* which compels them to faithfully respond to what needs their attention in the here and now. This requires an honest approach to experiencing.

In summary, here are the time perspectives for each type:

Enneagram Number	Dominant Perspective to Time	Supporting Perspective to Time	Repressed Perspective to Time
One	Present	Past	Future
Two	Present	Past	Future
Three	Future	Present	Past
Four	Past	Future	Present
Five	Past	Future	Present
Six	Present	Past	Future
Seven	Future	Present	Past
Eight	Future	Present	Past
Nine	Past	Future	Present

Conclusion

Time can be a curse. It can also be a gift. There is a parable attributed to many coastal communities throughout Latin America that explores this tension. It's called "The Fisherman and the Businessman", and it generally goes something like this:

> There was once a businessman who was sitting by the beach in a small Brazilian village.
>
> As he sat, he saw a Brazilian fisherman rowing a small boat toward the shore having caught quite a few big fish.
>
> The businessman was impressed and asked the fisherman, "How long does it take you to catch so many fish?"
>
> The fisherman replied, "Oh, just a short while."
>
> "Then why don't you stay longer at sea and catch even more?" The businessman was astonished.
>
> "This is enough to feed my whole family," the fisherman said.
>
> The businessman then asked, "So, what do you do for the rest of the day?"
>
> The fisherman replied, "Well, I usually wake up early in the morning, go out to sea and catch a few fish, then go back and play with my kids. In the afternoon, I take a nap with my wife, and evening comes, I join my buddies in the village for a drink — we play guitar, sing, and dance throughout the night."
>
> The businessman offered a suggestion to the fisherman.
>
> "I am a PhD in business management. I could help you to become a more successful person. From now on, you should spend more time at sea and try to catch as many fish as possible. When you have saved enough money, you could buy a bigger boat and catch even more fish. Soon you will be able to afford to buy more boats,

set up your own company, your own production plant for canned food and distribution network. By then, you will have moved out of this village and to Sao Paulo, where you can set up HQ to manage your other branches."

The fisherman continues, "And after that?"

The businessman laughs heartily, "After that, you can live like a king in your own house, and when the time is right, you can go public and float your shares in the Stock Exchange, and you will be rich."

The fisherman asks, "And after that?"

The businessman says, "After that, you can finally retire, you can move to a house by the fishing village, wake up early in the morning, catch a few fish, then return home to play with kids, have a nice afternoon nap with your wife, and when evening comes, you can join your buddies for a drink, play the guitar, sing, and dance throughout the night!"

The fisherman was puzzled, "Isn't that what I am doing now?"[10]

It's a well-known story, typically used as a lesson on contentment amid our urge to strive. But I also think it has something to teach us about time. Given the same amount of time, people can perceive what we are called to do with that time in vastly different ways. Perspective is important. Discernment isn't so much about finding more time (*chronos*; quantity). It's more about stewarding the time (*kairos*; quality) more faithfully. We are all prone to consider time from only one or two perspectives, keeping the third at bay. Bringing all three to bear on our exploration of vocation will provide essential wisdom and clarity.

The enneagram teaches us that our dominant number doesn't change. I can't simply discard my own Threeness to be a Type Six. If our number doesn't change, then our stance doesn't change either. However, this shouldn't cause us to lose hope, shrug our shoulders, sigh, and carry on as we always have. You can work to unveil the patterns of your dominant type. You can work to access your neglected perspective toward time. Aggressive numbers (Three, Seven, Eight) can cultivate *Sacred Delay* (past). Dependent numbers (One, Two, Six) can learn to develop *Sacred Vision* (future). Withdrawing numbers (Four, Five, Nine) can learn to cultivate *Sacred presence* (present).

Delay. Vision. Presence. Past. Future. Present. Together they provide the environment for the very *kairos* moments to explore the depths and potential of vocation.

Exercises:

Minutes vs. Moments

- Track how you spend time in a 'typical' 24-hour day (that includes a normal workday). Mark down how you spend the time in 30-minute increments.
    - How much of your day was spent on 'autopilot'…just getting by?
    - How much of your day was devoted to reflection or spiritual practice?
- Reflect upon your life and list what you believe to be the *kairos* moments in your life; those important trajectory-shifting moments where you gained significant clarity or insight.
    - What were the circumstances or contextual factors around each of your *kairos* moments? Were you spending time intentionally searching for clarity? Or did the *kairos* moments sneak up on you?

Dependent Stance (Ones, Twos, Sixes)

- Schedule some significant time this week to foster a *Sacred Vision* for your future. Use this time to go to a place that is comfortable to you, but NOT your work or home (a coffee shop or bookstore perhaps). When you are there, use the time to think and dream about the future, unattached from all the i's you'd like to dot and t's you'd like to cross beforehand. Give yourself permission to engage in this even if it seems messy, selfish, or unsure. Overall, if it feels indulgent, you're on the right track.

Aggressive Stance (Threes, Sevens, Eights)

- Schedule some time this week to foster a *Sacred Delay* to learn from your past. Go airplane mode on your phone and laptop and spend some time reflecting upon your past day, week, month, and year. Spend time pondering the question: What can I learn from where I've been? Also, try to be more in tune with the feelings that emerge in this time. Write them down. To the best of your ability, let them surface and dwell on them. If it feels unproductive, you're on the right track.

Withdrawn Stance (Fours, Fives, Nines)

- Commit yourself to cultivating *Sacred Presence* through faithful action this week. Give yourself a defined amount of time (30 minutes perhaps), to look ahead at your week and its responsibilities. Write down the things you need to do this week and what it would look like to be fully present in each responsibility. Then, go do it. If it helps, use "Sacred Presence" as a mantra to bring your focus to the present throughout your week. If it feels a bit tiring, you're on the right track.

Notes

[1] Melissa Gregg, "The Productivity Obsession," in *TheAtlantic.com*, November 13, 2015.

[2] Max Weber, *The Protestant Ethic and the Spirit of Capitalism* (New York: Penguin Classics, 2002).

[3] Mumford and Sons, "Awake My Soul," *Sigh No More* (New York: Glassnote, 2009).

[4] Annie Dillard, *The Writing Life* (New York: Harper Perennial, 1989), p. 32.

[5] *The New Strong's Greek Exhaustive Concordance of the Bible* (Nashville, Thomas Nelson, 2010).

[6] The concept of orientation to time originally comes from enneagram teachers Hurley and Donson, from their book *Discover Your Soul Potential*. Types One, Two, and Six, they claim, are oriented toward the present, Types Four, Five, and Nine to the past, and Types Three, Seven, and Eight to the future. (Associated with your "stance"). I initially learned of time orientation from Suzanne Stabile.

[7] Many Enneagram teachers since Karen Horney teach this approach. I first learned it from Suzanne Stabile, and have developed my own understanding through the works of Don Richard Riso and Russ Hudson.

[8] Check out Daniel L. Schacter, Donna Rose Addise, and Randy L. Buckners article in *Nature Reviews Neuroscience (8)*, 657-661, 2007. Retrieved from: www.nature.com/articles/nrn2213.

[9] As quoted in Bobbi Govanus' *Breaking Through: Reinventing after Failure* (Morrisville, NC: Lulu Press, 2017), p. 132.

[10] This particular version of the story comes from Paulo Coehlo's blog, http://paulocoelhoblog.com/2015/09/04/the-fisherman-and-the-businessman/.

The Way of Discernment

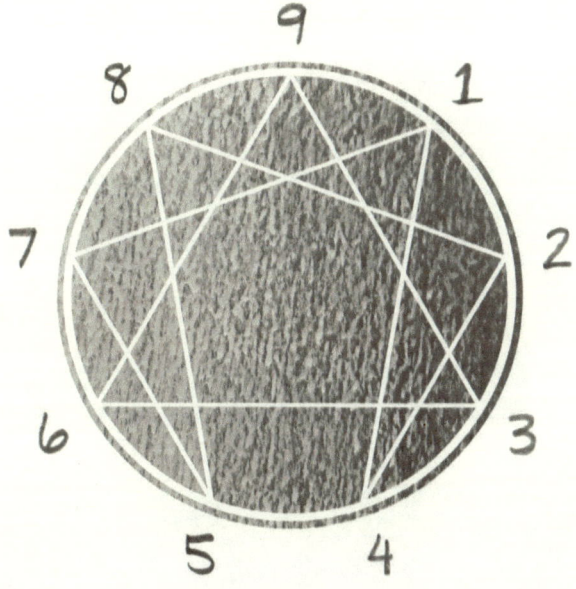

What I Mean When I Say...
(a brief review of key terms and concepts)

Adapted Self—an over-identification with our ego-centered personality. The persona we have developed to make our way in the world. Our adapted self helps us and hinders us. This is evidenced by our over-reliance on our enneagram type.

Authentic Self—the beloved self-in-God, made in the image of the Divine. Our authenticity reflects the *Imago Dei* (image of God).

Anger—a state of displeasure, annoyance, or hostility. The dominant emotion of the Gut Triad Types: Eight, Nine, and One.

Anxiety—the human response to stress in life. This is different than a clinically diagnosed anxiety disorder. Experiencing anxiety is a universal human phenomenon. Our responses to that anxiety vary by type, as evidenced by our dominant emotion.

Beloved—one who is completely covered and encompassed in love. By rediscovering our authentic self in the *Imago Dei*, we understand that we are beloved.

Discernment—the gift and practice of living our lives from a deep sense of vocation, with wisdom, in the fullness of time.

Ego—a psychological concept that is one of the three parts of psychoanalytic theory (along with the *id* and the *superego*). How you have learned to identify yourself. This when combined with our dominant enneagram type, forms the adapted self.

Fathom—The term "fathom" originally meant "outstretched arms," and was used in nautical contexts to measure the depth of where you were. Over time, "fathom" came to mean the way in which we understand a difficult problem or situation. It conveys a depth beneath the surface. We take the time to penetrate the surface, and, bit-by-bit, come to a place of deeper comprehension in order to better understand where we are going.

Fear—an unpleasant state caused by the belief that someone or something is dangerous, likely to cause pain, or a threat. The dominant emotion of the Head Triad Types: Five, Six, and Seven.

Flourishing—Our common purpose in the Vocation Triad. The proper translation of the ancient Hebrew concept of *shalom*. In the ancient Hebrew wisdom tradition, *shalom* means flourishing in the expanse of life. It's a call to live a life in right relationships with God, self, others, and creation.

Practice in Time—The Practice Triad in The Way of Discerning is an invitation to cultivate the fullness of time (*kairos* time) through wise engagement of the past, present, and future.

Shame—a state of painful negative thoughts about oneself; humiliation or distress caused by the experience of being wrong or foolish. The dominant emotion of the Heart Triad Types: Two, Three, and Four.

Vocation—The Vocation Triad in The Way of Discernment is an invitation to receive the Divine Call of identity, purpose, and direction.

Wisdom—The Wisdom Triad in The Way of Discernment is an invitation to engage and apply the three centers of intelligence: head, heart, and gut. This forms the holistic intelligence that guides us to engage our lives, and the many decisions therein.

CHAPTER FIVE

Type Four: "The Individualist"

"Empathy is the antidote to shame."
—Brené Brown

Fours want belonging but settle for longing.

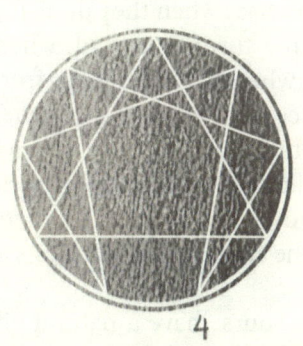

Type Fours are often labeled as individualists. While this describes some expressions of Fours, it doesn't capture what Fours are truly after. Fours, at their core, want belonging and connection. They want to belong, and they want the world to be marked by connection. But when confronted with a world that doesn't always make space for all as they are, it feels threatening. They can see need for belonging and connection everywhere, and they see it

most prominently within themselves. This leads Type Fours to feel anxious about life, and that stress manifests as a particular type of shame: deficiency. Because of their sensitivity to being truly known and accepted, deficiency takes on a more subtle and acceptable version: deep and extraordinary longing for connection. In order to keep the longing in check, Type Fours settle for secondary longings they conjure in their world: the extraordinary, the creative, and the unique. This results in Fours shunning the ordinary and mundane in search of re-establishing depth and connection. These small doses of uniqueness can confuse the inherent belonging of Fours, and feed their sense of deficiency or inadequacy. Fours' attunement toward being misunderstood drives this pursuit of the unique.

The Way of Discernment for the Type Four is to engage their dominant emotion, shame, in order to reconcile it. The shame that Type Fours carry is their most significant barrier. When Fours intentionally return to a place of belonging, significance, and wholeness, the components of the Way of Discernment (vocation, wisdom, practice) align to make good decisions.

In decision-making, Type Fours tend to perceive the options before them in their Heart Center, and feel a persistent sense of loss. The shame of what's missing compels them to respond in a few ways. First, they tend to isolate and retreat into the depths of their emotions. A Four's shame often arises when they don't feel that they belong, which can result in a turning inward, where they see more lack within. Second, when they reemerge from their cocoon, they present a uniquely crafted persona, much like a butterfly, that distinguishes them from the crowd in which they withdrew. In this way, their distinct presence in their world masks a self-consciousness about how they appear to others. Both responses are defenses against the anxiety that manifests as shame for Type Fours.

According to Beatrice Chestnut, Fours "have a natural gift for understanding the deeper emotional level of experience and seeing the beauty in darker emotions that other types would rather not feel, much less acknowledge."[1] The vividness of their emotional world, coupled with their shame, often leads Fours to feel like outsiders in their world. This is enhanced by a pronounced sense of idealism that saturates the Four's experience. They want to be in an ultimate and ideal world in which nothing is missing and everything belongs. My friend Seth Creekmore relayed to me a description of the Type Four he heard from enneagram teacher Leslie Hershberger: "Fours see the best of what's missing and the worst of what is present."[2] When integrated, Fours see the best of what is here and the form and shape of what's to come.[3] This develops a sort of push and pull dynamic in relationships, a tension of what is and what could be. Fours often draw people in on deep emotional levels. They also can push away out of fear that others can't handle or understand them. While confusing to other Types, this push/pull approach is a relational expression of the Four's living in the tension of belonging and longing.

This inner intricacy in Type Fours is one of the reasons why they are perhaps the least understood type of the enneagram. Often typecast as the "overly dramatic," they are simply better able to access the depth and breadth of their emotional world than the rest of us. In times of conflict, Fours can be emotionally reactive and wonder why other types aren't following suit. Relational tension can bring up shame and question their sense of belonging, which stirs the Four's emotional wells. When we question if Fours are being "too dramatic," perhaps we should question whether we are being dramatic enough. Beneath their expression is a deep ache to be known and understood.

Strength – Beauty and Meaning in the Journey

In seasons of discernment, Fours should be encouraged, for many of the skills and practices required for wise discerning are quite natural for them. Fours, when healthy and thriving, are attuned to their inner world in a way that naturally discerns. Their ability to plunge the depths of a situation allows them to see beneath the surface and through the superficialities of their world.

In this way, they have a way of recognizing, perhaps even manifesting, the beauty and meaning of the journey. This is why David Daniels describes Fours as having "a knack for making the ordinary extraordinary."[4] Seasons of discernment can be intense, saturated full of meaning and significance. Fours are poised for times such as this. They can naturally attach deep symbolism to things that other types wouldn't. They possess an aesthetic sensibility that appreciates and cultivates beauty in their midst. Fours are deep souls that long for the depth that discernment requires.

Because of their deep emotional wells, Fours often have a high capacity for empathy. As discernment often includes invitations into communal wisdom and insight, the empathic ability of the Type Four provides important opportunities for connected, generative belonging. This allows Fours to be safe, trusted confidants. In empathic modes, Fours can gain clarity about their own lives. There is a beautiful reciprocity in love: When we help others, we too are helped. Fours embody this.

Fours also have the ability to arrive at a place of unique illumination and clarity about decisions because of their inclinations toward imagination and creativity. They have an uncanny ability to let their idealism motivate them toward that which can seem impossible to other types. Their aesthetic sensibilities aren't simply for creating a unique look for themselves. They have an eye for the good and beautiful, and thus can tap into creative energies and pursuits that can unlock insight and wisdom.

A healthy Four is a wise, discerning person. Fours can access the depths of their emotions, connect emotionally with others, and imagine a good and beautiful future. Recall the difference between *chronos* time and *kairos* time (Chapter Four). Fours provide a unique and clear insight into how to live in *kairos* time. Trace a Four's longing to its source, and you'll find a desire to experience *kairos* moments. In these moments, Fours embody a sense of belonging and with equanimity, a calm and composed state that engages the ups and downs of life without being swept to places where they get stuck.[5]

Type Fours Engage:

When has your appreciation of beauty led you to a surprising place?

When has your search for meaning helped you make a wise decision?

Challenge – Stuck in a Drama that Never Unfolds

The longing that Fours experience in their adapted state is a perpetual focus on what's missing, a thirst that is never quenched. When their environment reveals what's presently missing, Fours will withdraw in an attempt to chase down the longing. For most Fours, this is a complicated experience, for the longing they experience has a certain attraction and repulsion.[6] They are simultaneously captivated and offended by it.

This leads to an unhealthy dependency on the experience of longing. Left unchecked, the longing becomes an end unto itself, rather than an invitation to reflectively listen to want and desire. When Fours retreat into their own shadow world, they develop an attachment to the emotional experience that prevents them from fully living in the present. The push/pull nature others experience when in relationship with Fours is thus a reflection of what's occurring within. This is enhanced by the phenomenon of *introjection*, an unconscious adoption of the ideas or attitudes of others. Fours succumb to introjection in a particularly unfortunate way. When unhealthy, their capacity for empathy shrinks. They assume that the void and the lack of belonging is really within. Ginger Lapid-Bogda describes this as "fully absorbing and internalizing negative information about themselves without discerning if the data is accurate."[7] This is the temptation of the Type Four: to internalize perceived negativity.

This is the challenge of the Four's emotional world. While they have a distinct ability to wade into the depths, they can easily remain there at their own detriment. The introjection hijacks external negativity and finds ample room within, resulting in unhealthy patterns and cycles of shame. This ramps up the Four's longing and further distances themselves from engaging the present.

Left unchecked, Fours can become embroiled in a drama that never unfolds, a life lived one climactic scene to the next, while the overarching narrative never advances. Darkness becomes more comfortable than light. It's thus understandable why Fours are drawn to experiences of melancholy, the sweet but unquenchable longing for what could be. Introjection convinces the Four that the sweetness of melancholy is all there is. Inclusion and satisfaction are seemingly unattainable to the unhealthy Four, for they believe that they are the ones who are missing, lacking, and deficient. The stagnant drama festers an envy that comes from a comparison trap: Unhealthy Fours view others in a more positive light than they view themselves.

The challenge for Type Fours on the Way of Discernment is to engage the drama of life with equanimity, a calm and composed state that doesn't require the roller coasters of life to feel alive. The unfolding nature of life is inherently dramatic, full of intensity, surprise, and emotion. Fours must be careful in absorbing that which is missing in their world, and viewing it as their own void. Wise decision-making requires the ability to see what is missing, and then fully show up to the present and engage any lack with clarity of identity, purpose, and practice.

Type Fours Engage:

Where in your life do you feel stuck in a drama that won't seem to end?

_____

When do you tend to absorb the negativity of the surrounding world?

_____

Vocation – Identity, Purpose, Direction

Type Fours struggle with viewing vocation as a sufficient call to action. To borrow from a parable of Jesus in the New Testament, Fours may receive the extraordinary gift of calling and "hide it under a bushel," (a bowl or basket), rather than let light shine throughout their world.[8] Receiving the gift and committing to the practice of vocation are intertwined and interdependent. The Fours' inward focus can be helpful in receiving the gift, but Fours must be careful that their inward focus doesn't come at the expense of outward practice.

Vocation also compels the Type Four to engage their tendency to self-scrutinize. Hearing the Divine Voice of love allows them to confront self-loathing. Shame dissolves in the face of love. If Fours' enter into activities of self-scrutiny, they have little energy left for discernment from a place of authenticity.

This disconnect between gift and practice is enhanced by the Four's tendency to operate in their world from a perspective that people don't understand them and therefore don't know them. This is why many Fours play to their uniqueness as a doubling down on their perceived difference. And all the while the voice of introjection can drown out the Divine Voice. The *Imago Dei* is a redemptive rebuttal to introjection, for if we are created in the Divine Image, we are understood and known from a place of goodness and wholeness. Internalized negativity is drowned out by the Voice of God.

The Way of Discernment for Type Fours begins with returning to an authentic identity which believes that they inherently belong for who they are. The Divine Voice is calling Fours to the ultimate place of belonging: love. When Fours acknowledge their inclusion, they can embrace their authentic being. Here the Four shows up fully in their world, for they no longer have to *do* authenticity (cultivate a unique persona) because they *are* authentic.

Type Fours Engage:

How do you let your perception of difference thwart your activity?

Who am I?–Identity for Type Four

The Way of Discernment Identity Statement for Type Four is:

> *"I am made in the Divine Image, and in the Divine Image there is no shame of being unknown or excluded. My belonging and significance is in who I am, not simply what I uniquely express."*

To live from this place of identity requires the Type Four to align longing with the truth of inherent belonging. Longing and belonging are linguistically similar, deriving from the same root. And, the only difference between belonging and longing is "be."[9] Longing conveys desire. Belonging conveys affinity. Longing is directed toward that which is beyond our grasp. Belonging is experienced in that which is in our midst. In the call of the Divine, shame is brought into the light and exposed for the lie that it is. Belonging counters inner scrutiny and perceived difference. When discerning, Fours must engage the question *Who am I?* This is the very question that cultivates their empathy from an authentic place of belonging.

First, Fours must become more aware of their Fourness. The Four's tendencies to withdraw, disengage, and introject lead toward inaction that keeps them stuck and can thwart discernment. Type Fours must acknowledge the persistent longing in order to begin the journey toward belonging. Their over-reliance on their uniqueness in comparison to others is a proactive defense against exclusion.

Second, Fours must acknowledge the Divine Voice that calls them beloved. That which is created and unique comes from a source. Fours can be so consumed with the tension of belonging and longing that they lose sight of the Divine Source of all belonging. From this source, our differences and unique expressions are not proof of our separation from others, but show the beautiful diversity in creation. You do belong. By showing up to the *Imago Dei* within, Fours are better able to reconcile their uniqueness and belonging.

Third, Fours must relinquish the adapted self. Fours, in their adapted state, can overplay uniqueness as a way to engage their longing. Here we encounter the difference between longing and letting go.[10] Longing is a refusal to let go of what might have been or what could be. In this way, the adapted Four is a fantasy self. Relinquishing this adapted self is terrifying, for it ramps up the shame that whispers that they are ordinary at best, inferior at worst. Relinquishing confronts the Fours introjection and opens them up to their authentic identity. Here the Four must practically and physically learn to listen to their longings to gauge whether their responses are from an adapted or authentic place.

Fourth, Fours must live from authentic self with humility. For Type Fours, humility from authenticity requires a relaxing of sensitivity toward being misunderstood. Left unchecked, the growing perception of being misunderstood can foster aloofness. True humility engages others with the Four's natural capacity for empathy rather than envy, which embraces the presence of uniqueness and common ground. Humility holds difference and belonging in tension. Here the Four can raise their awareness of how their body communicates this sensitivity (and needs to engage in relaxation).

Fifth, Fours must befriend themselves. For the Type Four, befriending the self means stopping cycles of self-frustrating. When Fours become entrenched in their longing, their attraction to melancholy becomes an imitation of self-care. In this way, they trade self-care for a form of frustrating self-indulgence. Self-care is a willingness to be happy and pursue joy, which is an affront to the Four's tendency to remain in the shadows, stuck in cycles of darkness as a defense against the fear of being happy.[11]

Sixth, Fours must live from authentic self with agency. From authentic identity, a Type Four's energy is redirected toward activity. From an inherent place of belonging, agency is activated. This authentic agency can reverse what Sandra Maitri calls the Four's tendency toward the "extinguishing of gratitude."[12] Instead, they live purposely from the generative gratitude of their inherent belonging and significance.

Seventh, Fours must intentionally continue to do all of the above.
The Type Four patterns of longing and withdrawing are well-established. Fours must be intentional and even vigilant in reclaiming their sense of belonging. With belonging and significance within, Fours can put the ego in its proper place, and flourish.

Why am I here?

From inherent belonging and significance, a Four's purpose in life clarifies, fostering a concern about the belonging and significance of others. Their introjection wanes, and makes way for them to be fully present in their world. The Four's adapted self seeks to remain in the shadows of life in a fixation on suffering. The Four's authentic self emerges to engage others as they work through their own shadows. Here the Type Four can channel their empathy toward flourishing to help others work through their suffering.

When Fours recognize the *Imago Dei* within, they live with purpose. In seasons of discernment, Fours can ask *Why am I here?* to remind them of their self-giving belonging, significance and empathy.

Where am I going?

Fathoming the depths of the Type Four's direction comes naturally. The Four's challenge lies in fathoming from a place of presence, not withdrawal. The tendency to retreat to their inner sanctum replaces the essence of fathoming: to measure the true depth of where you are in the world. This requires the Four to align their body, heart, and mind to the present to set a healthy trajectory.

When Fours fathom and engage their Gut Center, they can animate their presence in the world. They can show up fully in a world in which longing doesn't hold such power. Rather, the longing can become an embrace of the lack, freedom from the tyranny of what was or what could be. Their intuition is engaged, and their energy is focused toward action. They can use their ability to navigate the depths of their emotional world, and cultivate a beautiful and beloved community. To fathom this way, Fours should rest in solitude[13] to quell the persistent longing.

Type Four: "The Individualist"

In this way, rest and solitude transform the compulsion to withdraw and craft an authenticity. The image crafting gives way to a more authentic being.

Wisdom – Doing, Feeling, Thinking

In Chapters Three and Four we considered the Triads and Stances of the enneagram and how they employ the three centers of intelligence: doing, feeling, and thinking. Fours lead with feeling intelligence in their Heart Center, supported by thinking intelligence in their Head Center, but distort or misuse doing intelligence in their Gut Center. This leads to an overreliance on feelings and thinking.

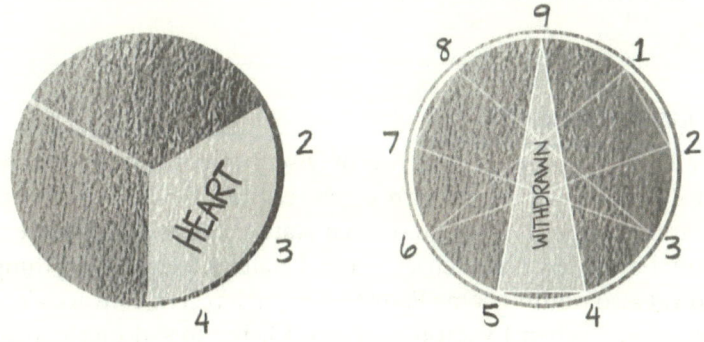

What am I doing?

Fours are keenly aware and interested in the depth and significance of their world, so it makes sense that they can struggle to see worth in the practical and mundane. Yet, most of our doing is engaging in practical and mundane matters. This affects Fours' motivation to do the routine. To ask *What am I doing?* helps Fours reflect upon their activity, or inactivity, to assess whether they are sufficiently showing up in their world. This helps Fours develop a check on their inaction, which often comes from a belief that they don't feel they can affect their environment.[14]

A much healthier approach for Type Fours is to activate their presence in the world by bringing their emotional depth with them and seeing it as a resource for their activity. This busts Fours' myth that they must work through their emotions before they can act. *What am I doing?* confronts this false dichotomy, and fosters healthy rhythms and alignment of doing intelligence with feeling and thinking.

Type Fours Engage:

What conditions typically need to be met before you act on something?

———

In what settings do you feel the most resistance to act?

———

What am I feeling?

Of all nine questions in The Way of Discernment, this is often the Type Four's favorite. Of all nine enneagram types, Type Fours are most aware of their emotional state.[15] Fours feel intensely. Many Fours describe their emotional state as feeling everything and yet also nothing. One Four I know, in a recent conversation, expressed, "When I want to feel sad, I listen to sad music, read dark poetry, etc." multiple times. The Type Four is not afraid of the emotional world, even when it leads to darker emotions.

When Fours ask the question *What am I feeling?* in The Way of Discernment, they must come to terms with their experiences of longing for what's missing, often that which they cannot name. Discernment raises this question in hopes of working through, rather than getting stuck in, the emotional space. This fosters a wise listening of the Four's longing, rather than a more compulsive submission to it.

For Fours to discern with wisdom, they must be aware of their attraction to experiences of melancholy. Their willingness to engage and explore their shadows is tremendously helpful in discernment. However, their comfortability in making a home there can be dangerous. For the Four, courage is evident when they are willing to leave the confines of their shadow world and step into the light of the here and now. Only then can the Four *integrate* dark and light.

What am I thinking?

Type Fours are prone to use thinking intelligence to analyze their feelings. This feeling-thinking combo fuels their tendency to withdraw, for analyzing the depths of the emotional world takes significant time and energy.

When a Four explores *What am I thinking?*, they assess the objectivity of the present use of their thinking intelligence. Fours have high capacities to employ their thinking toward what might have been and what would be. Riso and Hudson refer this to compulsion as "fantasizing."[16]

This causes Fours to struggle with objectivity. Their thinking is so closely tied with their feelings that sound judgment can be clouded. Left unchecked, a Four's thinking intelligence can be used to habitually intensify feelings.[17]

The Way of Discernment for Type Four is to disentangle their thinking from feelings in order to develop healthier, more objective rhythms of thinking intelligence. It's an invitation to the integration of thinking and feeling, as opposed to a form of enmeshment. From this integration, doing intelligence can be employed to enable the Type Four to engage with an active, grounded presence.

Practice in Time

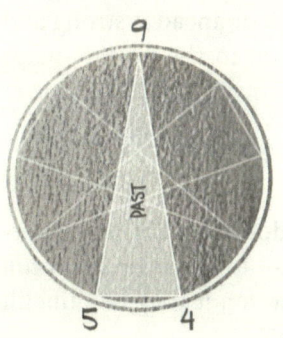

Type Four is a member of the Withdrawn Stance (See Chapter Three) along with Types Five and Nine. Withdrawn Types have a preferred past perspective on time, supported by a future perspective on time, while tending to neglect the present. This is evidenced by Fours willingness to withdraw to work through their feelings, longing for what was (past) or what could be (future). Both are compulsive reactions to longing, and a defense against engaging the present. Type Fours can translate the felt experience of something missing as a form of abandonment. This means that the searching for what is missing is more pressing than just about anything else in the present. Through practice, the Type Four can listen more attentively and objectively to the longing, in order to consider how to embrace the here and now (even when it lacks.)

This past orientation is supported by a tendency to circumvent the present to look into the future. In this way, the longing of a Type Four seems like an infinite line, extending into the past and future simultaneously. A nostalgic past and an idyllic future are comfortable ways to avoid engaging the present. Type Fours can cling to past events they believe were extraordinary, significant, or safe. They can also struggle to move on from past hurts. Fours also dream of fantastical futures rich in meaning, marked by belonging, free of shame. They are also just as able to imagine future scenarios marked by lack. The Four's ability to look back and ahead is sophisticated and complex.

Fours struggle the most to be fully present. In a way, showing up fully is a confession of belonging. One's presence is evidence of their perceived acceptance, that they are known and understood enough to feel safe and contribute. This is why Fours question whether or not they can truly affect their present environment. It's not so much a question of power, but membership.

To show up fully as one's true self in the here and now is a vulnerable and courageous act, one that Fours must engage to discern well. The temptation to look back or ahead is strong and often consuming. Intention and attention in the present helps Fours see the ways in which they belong, matter, and have power to engage the here and now.

What am I remembering? (Past)

The egoic patterns of the Type Four are dominated by a past perspective, so much so that Fours often fail to consider *What am I remembering?* Like a fish describing water, it may be difficult for a Four to reflect on this question. While it's accurate to say that Fours are prone to look to their past, it is also accurate to describe Type Fours as often being stuck in the past. This is especially true of painful past experiences. Fours can over-identify with past sufferings.[18] When unhealthy, Fours "may replace old hurts and disappointing experiences over and over again..."[19] How have these past experiences shaped who I am in the present? Am I clinging to things I should be letting go? How can my past sufferings cultivate empathy and love for those around me?

What am I experiencing? (Present)

If the Four's past is compulsive, the present can be overwhelming. If longing cannot be satisfied in the present, a Four can be quick to retreat. If being present is experiencing pain that is residual from the past, this is understandable. But from an authentic place of identity, a Four can honestly assess their experience, whether it be painful, exhilarating, boring, or extraordinary, and show up in their environment with agency and purpose. In this way, Fours can access their natural abilities of illumination and clarity. They can experience their present world with a depth and sight that discerns well.

To do so, the Type Four must experience the present not just in their Heart Center, but also in their bodies. By aligning their physical experience, their emotional experience, and their mental experience from identity and with wisdom, Fours can more keenly assess their present experience. At times, the present is marked with a noticeable lack, a missing piece of the puzzle. Often the missing piece is you. Belonging and significance are sometimes actualized by showing up and engaging as a leap of faith. Here longing actually can be a nudge to be present here and now.

> ### Type Fours Engage:
>
> What's your initial response to being fully present in an unknown situation?

How do you typically respond to situations in which you aren't sure you belong or fit in?

What am I anticipating? (Future)

When Fours consider their anticipation, they often can describe vivid narratives of what might or could be. It is here that the Fours' fantasizing tendencies tend to animate, imagining negative scenarios marked by lack (or even shrouded in darkness). Fours also develop ideal futures that help them escape from the present. The Way of Discernment invites the Four into a future grounded in reality, in which the past informs and the present activates. *What am I anticipating?* weaves the future together with the present in ways that minimize both extremes.

Discernment

Fours' abilities to see textures of life are a profound gift to discernment. Their appreciation for depth, beauty, and meaning are powerful resources. Their capacity for empathy gives them a unique ability to hold and steward others' pain. But these gifts are hindered when Fours experience shame as what they perceive they lack. Their sensitivity to difference and distance can isolate, further diminishing wisdom. When Fours cater to their perpetual longing, they can lose sight of who they are and *whose* they are. They can double-down on difference, discarding connection. Tragically, this can result in self-selecting out of groups, pre-determining that they don't belong. To discern well, Fours must be intentional with the following:

- <u>Identity Over Insufficiency</u>. The Type Four in an adapted state of persona is characterized by deficiency. It's what fuels the longing. The Type Four in an authentic state of identity is characterized by sufficiency. It's what eradicates shame and allows Fours to see their inherent belonging and significance. Make the identity statement for Type Four a mantra: "I am made in the Divine Image, and in the Divine Image there is no shame of scrutiny or lack. My belonging and significance are in who I am, not simply what I uniquely express."

- Wise Body. By intentionally engaging doing intelligence, Fours listen to their intuition to be actively engaged in their world. Living from Wise Body grounds Fours' feeling and thinking in their body rather than fantasizing in the past or future. In the Way of Discernment, the Four's feeling, thinking, and doing are integrated and aligned to engage the present with the many gifts they have to offer.
- Sacred Presence. Fours must practice Sacred Presence (Chapter Three) in order to discern their lives well. To show up fully is a bold admission that you belong and are significant. It acknowledges the role that the Four plays in satisfying the longing ever-present in our world.

Exercises for the Type Four Within

- Consolations and Desolations. In the Ignatian tradition (a stream of Catholicism) consolations and desolations are practices that cultivate deeper listening to the Divine. Consolations are those things that orient us toward God. Desolations are those things that orient us away from God.[20] Find helpful guides on this ancient practice from the Loyola Press website: www.loyolapress.com. Categorizing our life experiences in this way helps us more objectively discern our lives in light of the good and bad. Contemplatively spend a day or two in this framework. Next, take another two to three days considering the interplay of your consolations and desolations. How do your consolations and desolations each (or together) help you embrace lack (longing) and practice gratitude (belonging)? How do dark and light invite and teach?

- Practice Gratitude. Gratitude enhances a sense of belonging, for we develop connections to that which we are grateful. Take a week and commit to verbally giving thanks for anything worthy of it. Your gratitude should extend from the smallest of joys to the most extraordinary. If possible, keep a journal with you to document all that you are grateful for.
- Incremental Habits. The struggle to be fully present and employ doing intelligence poses a sometimes overwhelming challenge for Fours. Pick one or two habits that would increase your doing intelligence. Employ what James Clear refers to as the Atomic Habits technique,[21] incrementally increasing your doing in these one or two habits by 1% every day or two. Small wins will snowball into more complete action.
- Invert the Understanding Gap. Fours fall victim to the myth that others simply don't understand them and therefore can't really know them. This kicks the door open for introjection. Instead of focusing on other's lack of understanding, consider your own lack of understanding in a way that cultivates curiosity. Commit to two or three conversations with people which begin with you acknowledging, "I don't fully understand where they are coming from. How can I learn more?" This will foster the inherent empathy within you, and reveal how curiosity and connection can develop your own sense of belonging.

Questions for the Type Four Within

- Is this thing I'm doing now the thing I really should be doing?
- What emotions are warranted for this situation?
- What's mine to long for?
- How can my deep emotional wells be employed toward empathy for others?

Notes

[1] Chestnut, *The Complete Enneagram*, p. 268.

[2] Seth attributes this idea to enneagram teacher Leslie Hershberger.

[3] Thanks to my friend and Type Four K. J. Ramsey for this depiction.

[4] Daniels & Price, *The Essential Enneagram*, p. 33.

[5] Schafer, *Roaming Free Inside the Cage*, p. 106.

[6] Ibid, p. 104.

[7] Lapid-Bogda, *The Art of Typing*, p. 14.

[8] See Matthew 5:15 in the New Testament.

[9] Thanks to my buddy Seth Creekmore, who leads with Type Four, for this gem.

[10] Carolyn Bartlett, *The Enneagram Field Guide: Notes on Using the Enneagram in Counseling, Therapy, and Personal Growth* (Fort Collins: Nine Gates Publishing, 2003), p. 72.

[11] Chestnut, *The Complete Enneagram*, p. 280.

[12] Maitri, *The Enneagram of Passions of Virtues*, p. 141.

[13] Heuertz, *The Sacred Enneagram*.

[14] Hurley & Donson, *Discover Your Soul Potential*, p. 92.

[15] Riso and Hudson, *Discover your Personality Type*.

[16] This is Riso and Hudson's term for the mental fixation of Type Fours.

[17] Suzanne Stabile introduced this idea to in her compact disc recordings entitled *Enneagram and Discernment* (Dallas: Life in the Trinity Ministry).

[18] Calhoun, Calhoun, Loughrige, & Loughrige, *Spiritual Rhythms for the Enneagram*, p. 114.

[19] Chestnut, *The Complete Enneagram*, p. 276.

[20] You can find a good introduction to the Ignatian concept of con-

solation and desolation here: https://www.loyolapress.com/our-catholic-faith/ignatian-spirituality/discernment/discernment-consolation-and-desolation.

[21] Learn more about atomic habits from James Clear's website: https://jamesclear.com/atomic-habits.

CONCLUSION
Living the Way of Discernment

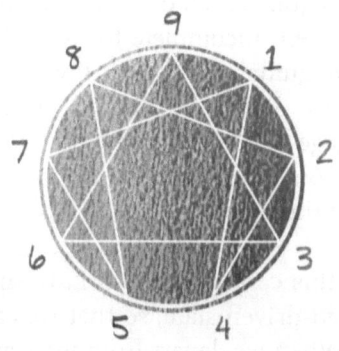

In the Introduction, I wrote about the power of a map. Granted, it's an odd illustration, for we hardly use maps anymore. Technology has rendered physical maps somewhat obsolete. But I've always found maps miraculous: a simple piece of paper can guide your steps in the world. They're practical and yet beautiful. Simple and yet intricate.

I proposed the Enneagram of Discernment to you as a "triadic map of applied identity." This particular map that you've held in your hands includes three such triads: Vocation, Wisdom, and Practice. I encouraged you to hold the map and learn to make sense of it.

For any map to be useful, you have to figure out where you are and plot your journey from there. Our dominant enneagram type is the trailhead to a deeper journey of discernment.

Type is simply the starting point. If we're willing to walk, we encounter the beautiful and brutal journey known as The Way of Discernment. Walking The Way helps us navigate the countless decisions that comprise a life. It's a pilgrimage of sorts, a sacred journey to discover who we are, why we are here, and where we are heading. There's a Latin phrase that captures this well: *solvitor ambulando*. Translated it means, "it is solved by walking." This is the profound truth of the enneagram and discernment. We discern by walking, beginning at the trailhead, and taking each next right step.

Here I must confess something to you. In my map-holding imagery, I intentionally withheld something from you out of fear of piling on too much, too soon. I must share it now, although you've probably discovered it yourself already. Holding the map of your inner life and making sense of it requires you to become a ***cartographer***. Cartography is the art and practice of drawing maps. This Way of Discernment requires each of us to draw the maps we hold, for they initially seem incomplete to us. We've found the trailhead, and we have guidance through the triads of Vocation, Wisdom, and Practice. But as we discover, learn, stretch, suffer, and grow, we engage in a cartography that connects the disparate experiences of our lives into a more coherent path. We connect the dots. We get the lay of the land. We can see the topography.

The enneagram helps us in this cartography work, raising our awareness of our adapted, ego-driven state, so that we can rediscover our authentic selves. When we depart from the trailhead, we learn what discernment truly means:

> *Discernment is the gift and practice of living our lives*
> *from a deep sense of vocation, with wisdom,*
> *in the fullness of time.*

Barriers to Invitations

Any honest journey to self-discovery engages our inner world in profound ways. In Chapter One, we explored our most significant barriers to discernment. These are the dominant emotions of the enneagram: anger, shame, and fear. By reading this book, I hope you discovered that The Way of Discernment transforms our most significant barriers into invitations. From authentic identity, purpose, and direction, our barriers invite us to engage our dominant emotion in loving and courageous ways.

Discernment is a way of seeing *beneath* and *through*. The Way of Discernment helps us see beneath and through our type's dominant barriers. Instead of running into them, and limping away bruised and confused, discernment helps us see what they may be inviting us into. They become holy biddings to listen, sense, consider, tend, and engage.

Anger, the dominant barrier of the Gut Triad (Types Eight, Nine, and One), becomes an invitation to flourishing action. Each type must discern its transformation of anger to action.

- The Type Eights need for protection is empowered in flourishing action that protects the most vulnerable in the world.
- The Type Nines need for peace is empowered in flourishing action that makes peace in the world.
- The Type Ones need for goodness is empowered in flourishing action to cultivate goodness in the world.

Shame, the dominant barrier of the Heart Triad (Types Two, Three, and Four), becomes an invitation to flourishing humility.

- The Type Twos need for unconditional love is empowered in flourishing humility to freely love others.
- The Type Threes need for value and worth is empowered in flourishing humility to cultivate the value and worth of others in their world.
- The Type Fours need for belonging and significance is empowered in flourishing humility to foster the belonging and significance of others.

Fear, the dominant barrier of the Head Triad (Types Five, Six, and Seven), becomes an invitation to flourishing courage.

- The Type Fives need for competency is empowered in flourishing courage to steward their knowledge for the sake of the common good.
- The Type Sixes need for loyalty is empowered in flourishing courage to intuitively trust themselves and bring others together.
- The Type Sevens need for contentment is empowered in flourishing courage to be content with what is, and what is within them.

With action, humility, and courage, we respond to the invitation of our dominant emotion. This doesn't mean future decisions will be easy. On the contrary, they may be more difficult. Integrity and authenticity has a more difficult time in today's world. It's often easier to approach decisions from our adapted, unaware self. Autopilot takes much less thought, emotion, and physicality than doing things manually.

When we engage life's decisions, big and small, The Way of Discernment provides the questions we need to ponder our steps forward with wisdom. When you face a decision and are unsure what to do, journey through the nine questions. For some, this can occur internally. For others, writing it out can be helpful. And for some, talking it through with a friend is best. Regardless, with a deeper understanding of your dominant enneagram type, considering these nine questions will engage vocation, wisdom, and the fullness of time.

The Vocation Triad

- *Who am I?*—Affirm your authentic identity. How does your identity as one made in the *Imago Dei* inform this decision?
- *Why am I here?*—Align your pursuits with your deeper purpose of flourishing (*shalom*). What options before you make way for flourishing? What options don't?

- *Where am I going?*—Fathom the depths of where you are, so you can more wisely discern where you are going. How can you fathom where you are so you can more clearly see the road ahead?

The Wisdom Triad

- *What am I doing?*—Sense what your body is telling you. Engage your instincts and intuition to assess your activity. Is my activity (or lack thereof) wise considering the options before me?
- *What am I feeling?*—Enter into the richness of your emotional world. Allow your feelings to teach you. What do your emotions have to say about the decision?
- *What am I thinking?*—Reflect upon your cognition. Consider how your thinking is helping or hindering your decision-making? How can you engage your brain to productively think your way through this decision?

The Practice Triad

- *What am I remembering?*—The past is a powerful teacher. We must be careful not to ignore it or wallow in it. How can memory help me engage this decision with wisdom? What should I be reflecting upon?
- *What am I experiencing?*—Our present engagement in the world is fraught with distraction and mixed messages. What are my gut, my heart, and my head experiencing in this decision-making process?
- *What am I anticipating?*—While the future is unknown, our ability to fixate on what could be, or fail to give ourselves permission to dream can radically impact our ability to discern. What do my anticipations tell me about the future I'm stepping into?

If we all journeyed through these nine questions, even briefly, consider the impact it would have on the quality of our lives, our relationships, our work, and our communities. Remember, we don't need more information. We really don't need any more knowledge. What we desperately need is wisdom to discern our individual and collective lives.

Go Back and Get It

The West African concept of "Sankofa" gives a concept for this type of discernment, capturing the essence of the journey. Sankofa is a mythical bird with its body forward and head turned backward. Roughly translated, "Go back and get it," the bird is a reminder that we must remember to fetch what is at risk of being left behind.

- SAN [Return]
- KO [Go]
- FA [Look, fetch]

Any work involving the enneagram and discernment is Sankofa work. We must go back and fetch what's at risk of being left behind: our identity, our purpose, our direction.

- SAN: We must return to our authentic identity as one made in the *Imago Dei*.
- KO: We must move forward with flourishing purpose, fathoming our direction.
- FA: We must engage our present in the fullness of *kairos* time, with head, heart, and gut aligned to cultivate wisdom.

This is the discerning life: *Sankofa* over and over again. As our dominant type doesn't change, our need to walk The Way of Discernment is lifelong. We will always have to go back and fetch what we risk leaving behind. We must give ourselves permission to take out our maps and consult them. The Jewish sacred text

Avot D'Rabbi Natan offers us an encouragement for this lifelong task: "Don't be afraid of work that has no end."[1]

Endless work can seem overwhelming. But it can also be evergreen. And that's a good thing. It's probably best that we perpetually and humbly receive the gift of discernment while consistently committing to its practice, over and over again. The ego will always want to shove its way to the fore and call the shots. The default patterns prowl. The dominant emotions lurk. This endless evergreen work is a lifelong practice of aligning and integrating our ego into our authentic self.

The Way of Discernment is no express lane. While it can provide momentary help in times of decision, it's a longsuffering journey. So, when the next decision comes, journey through The Way of Discernment. Hear the call to go back and get it, and discern your life with flourishing abundance. And do it over and over again, because it's worth it this way. You're worth it.

A Final Blessing

May your life be marked with the gift and practice of discernment.

May you see your dominant enneagram type as the trailhead to your inner landscape, and may you have the courage to take one step after another as a pilgrim journeying back to your authentic self.

May this pilgrimage include receiving the gift of vocation, the divine call to identity in the Imago Dei. *May it include invitations to practice your calling with flourishing purpose, fathoming the depths of the path that lies ahead.*

May you walk the path with loving wisdom through rhythms of Wise Mind, Wise Heart, and Wise Body.

May you discern your life in the fullness of kairos *time through the integration of Sacred Delay, Sacred Presence, and Sacred Vision.*

May it be so for you, and for us.

Notes

[1] Avot D'Rabbi Natan, https://www.sefaria.org/Avot_D'Rabbi_Natan?lang=bi.

ACKNOWLEDGMENTS

Writing an enneagram book truly takes a village, and I'm thankful to all the villagers who pitched in on this project to get me to the finish line.

My Family

Bekah—Your loving encouragement and challenge gave me healthy pauses (Sacred Delay) and sufficient hope. Thanks for putting up with a spouse consumed with the writing process. Plus, your copy-editing skills made the drafts less offensive to the English language. All my love.

My children—Ben, Isa, Sam, Stella, and Will, you make me want to be a better person in all the right ways. Thanks for your patience and forgiveness for all the times I had to shut myself in the office and write.

My Teachers

Suzanne Stabile—When I cracked open the door to peek into what a deeper study of the enneagram looked like, I came to you. You kicked that door wide open for me, and I'm grateful. Thanks for your wisdom, your Texan hospitality, and your love for the enneagram and your students.

Nan Henson—When I was searching for a place to deepen my studies, I never imagined Atlanta would be my enneagram home. What you are doing in the ATL, which reaches around the world, is simply beautiful. Thanks for your hospitable wisdom, caring disposition, and sweet brilliance.

Lynda Roberts—Your quiet strength and profound insight helped me engage parts of the enneagram in unexpected ways. I deeply appreciate the way you hold space for your students to be their true selves. Thanks for taking a chance with your certification program. May every cohort be packed with engaging students.

My Publisher

Dr. Keith Martel and the team at Falls City Press: Your belief in this project gave these words a home. When many "traditional" publishers were unwilling to take a chance on this "nontraditional" approach to the enneagram, you made room. May Falls City Press flourish in today's tumultuous terrain of publishing.

My Illustrator

Rachel Aupperle: Thanks for your brilliant and thoughtful work visually depicting so many of these concepts.

My Advisory Readers

It takes a pretty special group of friends to willingly sacrifice their time and energy to read my drafts and lovingly, yet firmly help me improve them.

My advisory readers group—Seth Abram, Seth Creekmore, Dr. Julia Hurlow, and K. J. Ramsey thanks for the many, many, many hours you spent wrestling with my words. I am truly blessed to call you friends, and this book is infinitely better because of your wisdom.

My type-chapter readers—It's a daunting and nerve-wracking thing to write about other personality types. Thanks for your grace, mercy, and wisdom in helping me better understand you and your fellow types. Seth Abram, Dr. Jeff & Rachel Aupperle, Kate Austin, Jordan Bolte, Hope & Jesse Brown, Seth Creekmore, Bill Cummings, Shelby Delay, Rachel Demarse, Whitney Drake, Hannah Goebel, Sara James, Dr. Julia Hurlow, Dr. Jerome Lubbe, the incomparable Bekah Moser, Chin Ai Oh, Amy Peterson, K. J. Ramsey, Jeremy Sims, Jake Smith, Kevin Smith, Amber Stanley, Kim Stave, Troy Tiberi, and Peter Yeung, I honor you.

My Fellow Enneanerds

Seth Abram, Seth Creekmore, and Kevin Smith—Thanks for your steadfast engagement and presence, even though we're all hundreds of miles apart. (Thank goodness for Marco Polo!) I'm grateful to learn so much from each of you.

Dr. Jerome Lubbe—Thanks for the late-night whiteboard sessions at your office. You helped refine my concepts in important ways.

Drew

APPENDIX

The Nine Questions of The Way of Discernment

Dr. Drew Moser

When facing a decision, and you're struggling to know what to do, consider the following...

The Vocation Triad

- Who am I? (Identity)
- Why am I here? (Purpose)
- Where am I going? (Direction)

The Wisdom Triad

- What am I doing? (Gut Center)
- What am I feeling? (Heart Center)
- What am I thinking? (Head Center)

The Practice Triad

- What am I remembering? (Past)
- What am I experiencing? (Present)
- What am I anticipating? (Future)

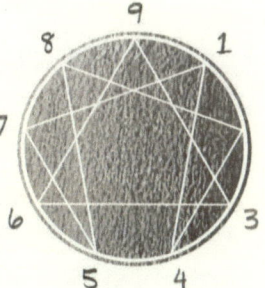

APPENDIX

Five Axioms of Discernment

Dr. Drew Moser

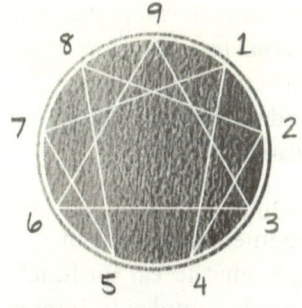

Discernment is one of those elusive ideas that's hard to describe, but we know it when we see it. The Latin root of the verb "to discern" means "to discriminate." In spirituality, discernment refers to the ability to sort out what is of God and what is not. Obviously, this is easier said than done. For *The Enneagram of Discernment*, the following five axioms of discernment help us better listen and see with depth and clarity:

Axiom 1: Discernment is a gift and a practice. Much of the spiritual life is the art of letting go so we can open ourselves: our minds, our hearts, and our bodies, to receive gifts from God. Discernment is one of those gifts. Often our ability to listen and see the depth and reality of what is, and respond faithfully, is a spiritual gift from God. Discernment is also a habit to be cultivated through intentional practice. Through our practice, we become more receptive to the divine gift. Much like an important conversation with a loved one, we receive such a conversation as a gift, and yet we also intentionally develop the habit of listening to our loved one well.

Axiom 2: Discernment requires self-knowledge, humility, and courage. In order to receive the gift and cultivate the habit of discernment, certain dispositions must be present. First, we must know who we are. Self-knowledge brings an honest assessment of our capacities and limits from a place of integrity. Second, we must receive the gift with humility, and allow humility to fuel our practice. Third, from a place of integrity and humility, we must embody courage to respond to the gift.

Axiom 3: Discernment is a process. Despite cartoonish notions of light bulb moments that instantaneously provide insight, discernment is much more of a process. It is the process of listening and living well, aligning interior movements with exterior action. It's a process of living from a place of internal freedom from making decisions based on selfish, ulterior, or unhealthy motives. Discernment cultivates awareness of God and the work of God in our present world in the contexts of solitude and community.

Axiom 4: Discernment is complex. Simple decisions don't require discernment. Mere choice or judgment will do. But discernment engages bigger questions than what to eat for lunch. Discernment is for deeper questions. Such complexity honors the depth of what matters most, and often leads us to explore other unforeseen questions. Discernment raises questions that beget other good questions. It is manifold and generative. Discernment acknowledges mystery, and is willing to explore it.

Axiom 5: Discernment is holistic. The process of discernment permeates our entire being: head, heart, and body. When we cultivate the ability to discern with wisdom, we learn to pay attention to our whole selves. This is how we see, as Nouwen would put it, "through appearances to the interconnectedness of all things." This is where true vision lies. Cultivating discernment draws from the intelligence available to us from our cognition, our emotional center, and our body awareness.[1] This holism also has a relational dimension. Not only do we discern from our entire being. We also discern from our interconnectedness with God, others, and creation.

Notes

[1] The Ignation concept of consolations and desolations is helpful here.

APPENDIX
Enneagram Settling Statements

Dr. Drew Moser

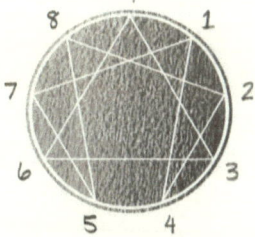

We too often settle for less than what we truly want.

The enneagram helps us become aware of the ways in which we project our core desires. When we project, we distort, and our core desires become cheap imitations of the real thing. It's a main pathway away from our Authentic Self to the Adapted Self, where the ego takes the reins.

We reason: "It's safer this way. It helps us get through our day."

But if we're honest, it's no way to live a life. If we simply settle, we'll always long for deeper things that our settling will never satisfy. Here are the Nine Settling Statements of the Enneagram.

Type 1—Ones want goodness but settle for order.

Type 2—Twos want unconditional love but settler for niceness.

Type 3—Threes want worth but settle for image.

Type 4—Fours want belonging but settle for longing.

Type 5—Fives want competency but settle for knowledge.

Type 6—Sixes want loyalty but settle for safety.

Type 7—Sevens want contentment but settle for excitement.

Type 8—Eights want protection but settle for control.

Type 9—Nines want peace but settle for calm.

APPENDIX
Nine Tips for Enneagram Typing

Dr. Drew Moser

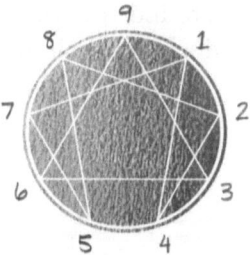

1. **Patience**—Be patient with yourself. Forcing yourself into a "type" doesn't work. This takes time.
2. **Read**—Pick up the time-tested enneagram books. Consider which description resonates the most, hurts the most, or feels the most unfair (or some combination of these three).
3. **Ask**—Ask those who know you well AND will steward such important conversations with love and grace.
4. **Listen**—Listen to all of the enneagram songs from *Sleeping at Last*. Pay attention to the song that makes you cry. If they

all make you cry, pay attention to the one that makes you UGLY CRY.

5. ***Listen Again***—Listen to all of the Enneagram podcasts from *Sleeping at Last*. Each episode dives deeply into an Enneagram song and includes profound descriptions of each type by Chris Heuertz.

6. ***Listen Yet Again***—Sit at the feet of a trusted Enneagram teacher in a live workshop. This is an oral tradition and learning from a master teacher can be incredibly helpful.

7. ***Focus***—Focus your attention on the small and big motivations that drive your behavior. They'll provide clarity.

8. ***Reflect***—Find pockets of time in your day to reflect on what's happening in your mind, your heart, and your body. What patterns emerge?

9. ***Relax***—Some take years to discover their dominant type. If you think everyone around you has everything figured out, you're wrong. They don't. We're all fumbling forward.

APPENDIX

The Nine Identity Statements of the Enneagram

Dr. Drew Moser

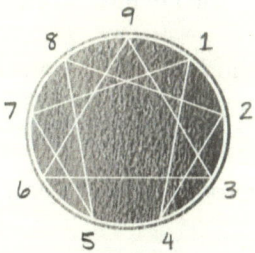

Type 1: "I am made in the Divine Image, and in the Divine Image there is no condemnation. My goodness is in who I am, not simply what I improve."

Type 2: "I am made in the Divine Image, and in the Divine Image there is no shame of being unlovable. I am loved and appreciated for who I am, not simply what I do for others."

Type 3: "I am made in the Divine Image, and in the Divine Image there is no shame of being worthless. My worth and value are in who I am, not simply what I do."

Type 4: "I am made in the Divine Image, and in the Divine Image there is no shame of being unknown or excluded. My belonging and significance is in who I am, not simply what I uniquely express."

Type 5: "I am made in the Divine Image, and in the Divine Image there is no fear of incompetency or depletion. My competency and viability are inner renewable resources to be shared with others."

Type 6: "I am made in the Divine Image, and in the Divine Image there is no fear of being alone. Support and guidance is within, not simply in what I can secure."

Type 7: "I am made in the Divine Image, and in the Divine Image there is no fear of lack. My contentment is in who I am, not simply what I can plan or experience."

Type 8: "I am made in the Divine Image, and in the Divine Image, anger is refined.
My protection is in who I am, not simply what I control."

Type 9: "I am made in the Divine Image, and in the Divine Image, anger is resolved.
My peace and wholeness is in who I am, not simply in what I keep calm."

APPENDIX

Nine Stages of Enneagram Learning

Dr. Drew Moser

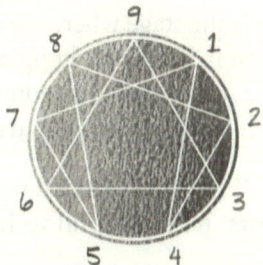

The Way of Disorientation

- Stage 1-CONFUSION | "What is any-gram? Never heard of it."
    - While easy to understand this stage, it's important to remember that we all start our journeys here. All of us experienced a moment in which we first heard about the enneagram. Remembering this point is an important perspective as we follow the path.

- Stage 2-SKEPTICISM | "This enneagram thing is garbage. I don't know why everyone is so obsessed with it."
    - You may scoff at the naysayers, but it's important to honor this step. It's a natural response to encounter something new and strange to us with skepticism.

- Stage 3-RESIGNATION | "Fine. I'll look into it. It's all anyone is talking about so I might as well give it a go."
    - At this stage, it's critically important to honor the wisdom of the enneagram AND the person who is willing to explore it. We must tend to both with care.

The Way of Discovery

- Stage 4-WONDER | "Holy crap! This thing reads my mail!"
    - This is the stage where we begin to be truly honest in acknowledging our dominant type. Once we see how our dominant type explains so much of what motivates us, we sit in wonder.

- Stage 5-SIMPLISM | "I read a few books and listened to some podcasts. It's so helpful to have everyone I know figured out."
    - At this stage, we begin to turn our working knowledge of the Enneagram toward others. It becomes a lens through which we make sense of the world. Unfortunately, it's a simple lens that, left unchecked can lead to stereotyping and weaponizing the enneagram.

- Stage 6-EVANGELISM | "The enneagram is everything and I have to tell everyone about it."
    - Almost coinciding with Stage 5 is an evangelistic fervor of Stage 6. The Enneagram becomes

the THING we talk about in social settings. At this stage books and podcasts are PASSIONATELY recommended.

The Way of Descent

- Stage 7-COMPLEXITY | "The more I learn about the enneagram, the more I realize how little I know."
    - If we're honest, once we think we've reached the limits on this framework, new questions emerge. This stages requires a 'learned humility' that recognizes there's always more we can know.

- Stage 8-SUFFERING | "The deeper I get into this thing, the tougher it gets confronting my own stuff. Real inner work is hard."
    - If the enneagram is simply a way to label yourself and others, then there's no change. Those who stick with the work that the enneagram can provide find a painful, but worthwhile path of acknowledging and naming the darker parts of ourselves. This stage of the journey is the type of suffering that refines us.

- Stage 9-GROWTH | "The enneagram doesn't do the work of growth for me. It helps me realize my blind spots, where I need to let go of things, and where I need to change habits and practices. The rest is up to me."
    - At this stage, we recognize that the enneagram isn't everything. It's incredibly helpful, but only to the extent that we are willing to engage what we learn with attention and intention. The enneagram gives language and light to many parts of who we are, but it's up to us to cultivate the habits and practices for lasting growth.

APPENDIX
Recommended Enneagram Resources

Books (An Initial List)
- *Discovering Your Personality Type: The Essential Introduction to the Enneagram,* by Don Richard Riso and Russ Hudson
- *Discover Your Soul Potential: Using the Enneagram to Awaken Spiritual Vitality,* by Kathy Hurley and Theodorre Donson
- *The Complete Enneagram: 27 Paths to Greater Self-Knowledge,* by Beatrice Chestnut
- *The Essential Enneagram: The Definitive Personality Test and Self-Discovery Guide,* by David Daniels and Virginia Price
- *The Road Back to You: An Enneagram Journey to Self-Discovery,* by Ian Morgan Cron and Suzanne Stabile
- *Roaming Free Inside the Cage: A Daoist Approach to the Enneagram and Spiritual Transformation,* by William M. Schafer

- *Spiritual Rhythms for the Enneagram: A Handbook for Harmony and Transformation*, by Adel and Doug Calhoun, Clare and Scott Loughrige
- *Whole Identity: A Brain-Based Enneagram Model for (W)holistic Human Thriving*, by Jerome Lubbe

Websites

- International Enneagram Association – https://www.internationalenneagram.org/
- The Enneagram Institute – https://www.enneagraminstitute.com/
- The Narrative Enneagram – https://www.enneagramworldwide.com/
- Integrated Enneagram – https://www.integratedenneagram.com
- Enneagram Indiana – https://www.enneagramindiana.com

Podcasts

- Fathoms | An Enneagram Podcast, featuring Seth Abram, Seth Creekmore, & Drew Moser
- The Real Enneagram Podcast by Dr. Joseph Howell
- The Enneagram Journey Podcast with Suzanne Stabile
- Do it for the Gram: An Enneagram Podcast by Milton Stewart
- Typology with Ian Morgan Cron

Other Books by Dr. Drew Moser:

Scholarship Reconsidered [Expanded Edition]

Ready or Not: Leaning into Life in Our Twenties

Campus Life: In Search of Community

Follow Drew's Work:

www.drewmoser.com
www.enneagramindiana.com

Fathoms | An Enneagram Podcast

Twitter: @drewmoser
Facebook: www.facebook.com/drewmoserauthor
Instagram: @drewmoser // @enneagrammers

Booking Inquiries: drewmoser@gmail.com

Made in United States
Troutdale, OR
02/26/2025